No Sugar Added!

No Sugar Added!

One Family's Saga of Dementia and Caretaking

Shannon Lucid

Copyright © 2019 Shannon Lucid
All rights reserved.
ISBN 978-0-578-49541-5

Table of Contents

Forward vii

Chapter 1 1

Chapter 2 24

Chapter 3 40

Chapter 4 59

Chapter 5 90

Chapter 6 107

Forward

This is the book that I wanted to read when I realized that I was going to be hiking down the Dementia Trail with my husband, Mike. This is the book I needed that told about the hard reality of the journey. A book like this did not seem to exist, so Mike and I—and the rest of the family—stumbled along as best we could, hoping against hope that we would not get entangled in a chaotic maze of no return.

There are many books about dementia, but I found none that talked about the hopelessness of the daily grind of caretaking. I found none that talked about the big questions: what it means to be a Christian with dementia, a demented child of God, and a demented person created in God's own image. I found that none talked about what it means to care for such a person. This book does.

This is the story of one family's experience. It is a unique experience. But then, every demented family's journey is unique. I hope that knowing what others have thought and done—as well as understanding that God does not hide from those with dementia, but that God is with them every step of the way—is comforting to other families on the journey.

This is not a *Dementia for Dummies* book. It does not give detailed lists of what to do when. This is not a "Hallmark moment" book that ends with a loving relative squeezing the hand of a demented person in a care facility and seeing the "spark of God" flash momentarily in their eyes. This is a book of changing diapers, mopping floors, doing laundry, and discovering in so many ways that—no matter what—God does not forget the demented or those who love them

Chapter 1

2004–2007: The Beginning

We do not know what to do,
But our eyes are on you
—Jehoshaphat's prayer, 2 Chronicles 20:12b

"Sorry, your credit card was rejected," intoned the bored clerk at Walgreens.

That simple statement forced me to acknowledge that my husband Mike and I were truly on a fearful, tumultuous, unknown—but not godforsaken—journey of no return into forgetfulness and the loss of personhood.

I immediately went home and called the credit card company. Their answer to denial of payment was straightforward.

"The charge was denied because no payments have been made for several months," the person on the other end of the line told me.

Lucid

I said, "Thank you," as I looked around at the chaotic mass of papers in Mike's study.

It was time for action. Step one: stop excusing Mike's behavior with comments like, "We are all aging," or "Guess Dad is having a difficult time with retirement." Step two: acknowledge that Mike was—and had been—slowly sliding into a bizarre landscape devoid of navigational aids to help the rest of the family to either find or follow him.

In retrospect, the first dementia signs appeared before his retirement.

Late one evening, Mike went to pick up our son Michael at Hobby Airport in Houston. When Michael walked into the house, his first words to me were, "Don't ever send Dad to pick me up again. His driving is really scary."

I was trying to get a manuscript ready to send out to *Scientific American* about the six months I had spent on the Russian space station Mir. Ever since I had known him, Mike had always been the best editor for anything I had written. He had proofread my PhD thesis, "Effect of Cholera Toxin on Phosphorylation and Kinase Activity of Intestinal Epithelial Cells and their Brush Borders" to the point that when I turned it in to the school's thesis editor, she did not find any language errors at all. Mike was a nitpicker for details. For example, one evening when our oldest daughter, Kawai, was in high school and trying to get a paper ready to turn in the following day, she had her dad read it. He found an extra letter in one word. Kawai burst into tears of frustration. She ran into her room, yelling, "Why does Dad always find every single mistake!" (This was back in the days when a mistake meant painfully retyping the entire page on a typewriter, not just clicking a button and then reprinting). This time, after reading my manuscript, all he said was, "Seems OK." Even I, of minimal proofreading skills, knew that could not be true!

No Sugar Added!

The Shell Oil Company, where Mike had worked for more than thirty years, was reorganizing. Mike was asked to take early retirement. It was good from the standpoint that it was time for him to stop commuting. (By then the entire family had concurred with Michael's assessment of Mike's driving.) It was bad because it shattered the little self-confidence he had remaining. On his last day of work, he packed his car with boxes of papers from his office, stopped by the local storage rental place, rented a unit, stuffed it with his overflowing boxes of papers, and locked it—never to return. He then came home and sat.

Every day, Mike sat at home while I went to work. He sat in his study, surrounded by mounds of papers. Flyers that came in the mail were added daily, and nothing was ever thrown away. He had paper receipts overflowing from shoeboxes. Being at home, he of course got to the mail first every day. Every piece of paper in the mail made it into the collection in his study. None ever went into the trash. (Since we have all by now gone paperless, it can be hard to remember just how much paper could accumulate back in the days before automatic payments.) Mike was content sitting in the midst of his papers. He said that he was paying the bills. He had always paid the bills. That was his thing, and I had always been happy to have him do it.

After his early, forced retirement, Mike never worked in the yard, never cooked a meal, and never did any of the carpentry projects he had planned to do after his retirement. He was still vaguely talking about what he was doing on his various church committees. I encouraged him to continue being involved with the church. Before almost every committee meeting, he said he was too sick to go. His head hurt, his feet hurt, or his stomach hurt. The pastor called me at work. "Please get Mike to give up his position on the mission committee," he said. "Have him concentrate on getting better and then come back." That evening, I told Mike it was time for him to resign from the mission committee. He cried and then sent in his resignation.

One day, my daughters and I were surprised when we opened the trunk of Mike's car and found it full beyond capacity with packages of new garbage bags. Evidently, Mike had bought them from a student selling them to raise money for a school activity. And then, another time, there was the thousand-dollar check given to a random man who rang the front doorbell and convinced Mike that if he wrote a check to cash, the man would replace the chain-link, backyard fence. The check was cashed, but the fence was never replaced.

Our anniversary was in December, and my birthday was in January. For all our married life, Mike had given me roses on these occasions. The year before Mike was diagnosed with dementia, there had been no roses. But then came February. Mike went to the grocery store to buy some eggs. He returned without the eggs, but he was carrying an oversize basket of tulips. He handed the basket to me with a huge grin. Puzzled, I took them as Mike said, "I know how much you always enjoy roses for our anniversary, so I got these roses for you." He was clearly very happy and pleased with himself for giving me an "anniversary" surprise. What could I say but "Thank you"? Later, when thinking back to clues I had received but not acted on, I labeled that day "The day when tulips were roses."

Mike complained of many different physical ailments. He kept telling me that he was too sick to do this, or he didn't feel well enough to do that, so I got him an appointment with our family doctor. The doctor listened to the litany of complaints and then referred him to numerous specialists. I made appointments and drove Mike to them all. We went to an endocrinologist, a gastroenterologist, and a podiatrist. On the way home after having his blood drawn, Mike said, "I feel better already. It is really good to get rid of all that extra blood."

None of the doctors we'd seen or the tests he'd had found a problem.

I asked the family doctor for a referral to a neurologist. When we arrived at the neurologist's office, the doctor asked, "What is the presenting problem?"

"Mike is having problems remembering things, and he has not been paying the bills," I said.

Mike was sent for a CAT scan, and he answered the phone when the neurologist called a few days later with the test results. Mike listened and then muttered into the phone, "Tell my wife; I can't understand what you are saying." I took the phone.

"I was explaining to your husband that it appears he has vascular dementia," the neurologist told me.

"How does vascular dementia compare to Alzheimer's?" I asked.

"Vascular dementia is different from Alzheimer's in that with Alzheimer's, the loss of ability generally progresses a steady rate, whereas with vascular dementia, there will be plateaus of consistent ability, but then there will be a sudden drop. The person with vascular dementia will be at a new, lower level of functionality for a period of time before experiencing another decrement."

"Well, vascular dementia sounds better than Alzheimer's," I commented, meaning that it sounded like to me that there would be periods of stability rather than steady decline.

"Well, I guess if you want to think of it in that way, you can," the neurologist replied.

"OK. So, what do we do now?"

"I recommend going to a neuropsychiatrist for cognitive functionality testing. I will also prescribe Aricept for Mike to try. It is really for Alzheimer's, not vascular dementia, but it wouldn't hurt to try it."

Lucid

I started Mike on the Aricept. A couple of weeks after he had started it, I was out of town. Mike called my daughter while crying and screaming with cramping pain in his legs. She called the neurologist and was told that this was a side effect of Aricept and to discontinue the drug. We did.

An interesting side note is that more than a year after we had seen the neurologist, I got a call from her office saying that our bill had not been paid, and that it was being turned over to a collection agency.

I asked, "But didn't Medicare or Blue Cross pay it?" and was told that the bill had gone back and forth between these two agencies, but neither would pay. The neurologist's office said that numerous bills had been sent to Mike, but there had been no response from him.

I said, "He went to the doctor with a presenting symptom of not paying bills! I was not informed until it was time to call the collection agency?"

Mr. Lucid is the patient and did not give permission for someone else to receive the bills."

I then talked to Medicare and Blue Cross. The time limit for paying had passed while they were sending the doctor's bill back and forth to each other to see whose responsibility it was to pay it. I ended up having to pay the bill myself.

****

Our third granddaughter, Paige, was born on February 17, 2004. We left the hospital that morning where we had held her for the first time and went directly to the neuropsychiatrist's office to hear the results of the cognitive tests Mike had taken two weeks previously. The psychiatrist said that the results of the testing showed that Mike was cognitively impaired. He also said that Mike seemed a little depressed and that he would be glad to have Mike come in for counseling sessions to help him cope with this new phase of his life.

I wanted to reply, "Well, wouldn't you be depressed, too, if you were vaguely aware that you were losing cognitive abilities and memory? How do you think counseling would reverse the damage done by breaking blood vessels?" But I didn't. Instead, I just said, "Thank you." We left. I knew that I would never be able to get Mike to agree to return for any counseling sessions.

Mike and I left the doctor's office without saying anything to each other. We walked to the parking lot and then stood together in silence beside the car. Both of us were dimly aware of the fissure starting to open between us, separating the cared-for from the caregiver, the remembering from the un-remembering. In that instant, neither of us really comprehended how this gap between us would open into a gargantuan chasm that would sever all possibilities of shared communication—a chasm leaving all shared memories on one side, with one person holding them all and the other person holding none. This memory chasm would prove to be much greater than the final chasm between life and death.

Silently, we got into the car and drove back to the hospital to be with our newest granddaughter.

That day, we witnessed the juxtaposition of a beginning and an ending of personhoods. Paige was at day one and Mike was at day 24,466 (sixty-seven years). The rejoicing over every bit of evidence of a new personhood emerging while grieving over every evidence of a person disassembling started me obsessively pondering this paradox and asking what it means to be a person. Is there a precise point when a person becomes a nonperson? What does it mean for a Christian to no longer know that he or she exists? What are the responsibilities of those who remember and love a person when that person starts to dissolve? What is the responsibility of the church and the Body of Christ to those members when they no longer know that they are part of the corporate body? What is personhood? What does it mean to be a person? That day, I started a self-initiated, self-directed, all-consuming crash course entitled, "The Philosophy of the Mind: Philosophical and Ethical Assumptions About What Is Meant by Personhood."

****

Soon after the diagnosis of Mike's vascular dementia, I attended the funeral of a neighbor's mother who had died of Alzheimer's. The pastor read:

> *For I am convinced that*
> *neither death nor life,*
> *neither angels or demons,*
> *neither the present nor the future,*
> *nor any powers,*
> *neither height nor depth,*
> *nor anything else in all creation*
> *will separate us from the love of God that is in Christ Jesus our Lord.*
> —Romans 8:38–39

The pastor then made the point that it did not matter if a person knew who they were or not. God remembered them—and nothing, even the total absence of memories, could separate you from the love of God.

And there it was: God's promise. Nothing could separate Mike from the love of God. The total disintegration of Mike as a personality, the total loss of any knowledge of family or of God, and even the loss of any knowledge of being a human being—none of these could separate Mike from God's love. God's love for us was not dependent on our being able to remember the existence of God or to remember the existence of who we are. God knew. God remembered. And God loved us.

Over time, the realization dawned on us—Mike's family—that in caring for Mike, we were the hands and feet being used by God to daily reassure Mike that he was not forgotten by God, and that he was not separated from the love of God.

This was the starting place of finding answers to the tumultuous questions birthed by Mike's diagnosis of dementia. This was the bedrock of a promise upon which we built eleven years of caring for Mike. I decided that I would name Romans 8:38–39 "Prayer for All Caretakers of the Demented." I discovered that this constant reminder of the presence of God's love brought great comfort to me, the caretaker, as I cared for Mike, the demented. God promised.

****

For the first few years after the flurry of doctors' appointments and Mike's formal diagnosis of vascular dementia, life just continued on. I still kept going to work every day. Brianna, our fourth granddaughter, was born three months after Paige was born, and our daughters, Kawai and Shani, both stayed at home to take care of their infants and toddlers. Fortunately, especially for my sanity, they both lived very close and were readily available to help me. This made them rapidly become very adept at crisis management. I bought a huge swing set for the backyard because I wanted the grandkids to view spontaneous trips to visit Grandpa as a real treat. It worked. It was just too bad that Kate leaped out of a swing the second week it was there, landing on both hands and breaking both arms. Searching for a silver lining, we decided that

Lucid

the twin blue casts on her arms did nicely bring out the blue of her eyes!

We—Mike's family—settled into a flexible lifestyle of constantly trying to adjust to the relentlessly ever-decreasing plateaus of functionality that Mike landed on. Maybe it was either our imagination or wishful thinking, but there did seem to be periods of stable functionality that we adjusted to, and each time we figured that this was the new normal. The problem was that we were always playing catch up, lagging three steps behind Mike's changes. We were always looking in the rearview mirror of our existence, and for eleven years we marked each drop to another plateau with the exclamation, "We really did not know that things could get this much worse! We did not know how good things were two years back, or how easy it was to care for just Mike three months ago!"

Most of the time, we lulled ourselves into believing that things were OK, but then there would be an incident that once again told us that nothing would ever be OK again.

Soon after Mike was diagnosed, he would get very frustrated when he didn't remember the name of an object. We blitzed the house with sticky notes with the name of the object that it was stuck to printed in large letters on each note. Mike angrily yanked them off. Not being able to figure out why, we gave up on that idea when we tired of picking sticky notes up off the floor. Every day when I left to go to work, I posted signs around the house with the name of the day and signs saying where I was. For his sixty-eighth birthday, I gave Mike a big clock that told the day of the week instead of the time. But if I was not at home and someone asked Mike where I was, he never knew.

Seeing the mail truck parked on the street threw Mike into a frenzy, so the front blinds were always kept closed.

During this time, there was an altercation between Mike and the lawn service people. Neither the girls nor I were home, so we never knew what really happened. The easiest solution—and we always went with the easiest—was to start once again mowing the lawn myself.

Mike never lost the ability to surprise me—and not in a good way—when I came home from work.

There was the day that I came home from work and found Mike, his face a bright red, sitting at his desk and yelling at his computer, angry beyond angry. He saw me and shouted that he had never said that the phone could be disconnected. I saw that the phone cord had been pulled out of the wall. Discreetly, I reconnected the phone and said everything was OK. Fortunately, right at that time, Amberle, and Brianna arrived with their dad, Kirk. Seeing the grandkids diffused Mike's anger. I moved Mike's desk so that the phone cord could no longer be yanked from the wall. No memory aids, no matter how creative we thought they would be, helped orient Mike to the present.

****

We had many discussions about Mike continuing to drive. We still had no solution when Mike solved that problem on his own, without our needing to intervene.

One Saturday morning, Mike said that he was going to drive over to church for a meeting. I watched him back out of the driveway. Fifteen minutes later, he was back in the kitchen.

"That was a quick trip," I said.

"I did not go," he replied.

"What happened?"

"I got to the light at Highway 3 and Clear Lake City Boulevard. I did not know where I was going. I was very scared. I came home."

Mike never drove again. From then on, I always drove when we got in the car together. And just to make sure that he did not drive

Lucid

when I was not at home, I disconnected the battery cables of his car and hid the keys. But just in case, to be sure all bases were covered, I left him as a driver on the car's insurance.

Then there was the hot, Texas, summer day when I walked into the house and found the cage of Oscar, our African gray parrot, empty. I searched for him all over the house. Mike helped me. I gave up the hunt and then went into the garage to get a roll of paper towels. I just happened to look into Mike's car, which I always kept in the garage to keep Mike from driving. There was Oscar, sitting on the steering wheel and looking overheated. Mike and Oscar had always had a special bond. For instance, when Mike placed him there, Oscar would stay perched on Mike's shoulder until Mike placed him elsewhere, as they wandered together around the house. Mike must have "wandered" into the car and placed Oscar on the steering wheel. A few days later, I came home from work, looked for Mike, and found him in the garage, locked in the same car, minus Oscar, with the windows rolled up, gripping the steering wheel and crying. Being locked in a closed vehicle in the Houston summer heat is good for neither man nor beast. It was time to get rid of Mike's car. I donated it to a charity. A tow truck arrived, loaded up Mike's car, and then drove away. During this entire process, Mike stood by the door that opened onto the driveway and sobbed. As soon as the tow truck was out of sight, however, Mike stopped crying and never mentioned the car again. Out of sight, out of mind. But not for me. I could not, cannot, shake the image of Mike standing, sobbing at the door. I continued and continue to cry.

****

After credit cards not being paid and the electricity being cut off (trust me—it is a real shock to call the electric company to report

No Sugar Added!

no service and to be told that you haven't paid your bill in forever!), I realized that, like it or not, I was going to have to take over our finances. It was hard, not only because I had a steep learning curve but also because Mike thought he was still in charge of paying the bills, even though he was not doing anything except losing them. From the beginning of our marriage, Mike had always been in charge of the finances. He had been a little aghast soon after we got married when he found out that I had always just kept my bank balance in my head. He liked to know—down to the penny—what happened to our money. I couldn't care less so, for us, it had always worked out well that he took care of all the bills.

Our daughter Shani and her husband Jeff set it up so that our bills could all be paid online. That solved the problem of Mike getting to the mail and then losing it before I got home. Mike never noticed that the bills stopped coming in the mail and did not realize that I was paying them online.

I got a call from the church treasurer, who asked if I knew that Mike had written an eight-thousand-dollar check to the church the previous Sunday. I said no, and that I would take care of it. I went to the credit union where my paychecks were deposited and took Mike's name off the account. That made me feel very guilty and sad. After all, during all the years of our marriage, we had always shared everything, but I could not risk him writing another large check. I hid all the blank checks to his account. He never asked about them—I guess that not seeing the checks, he never thought about writing one.

One day, a statement came for one of his IRAs. He held the paper all day and kept insisting that it was from the wrong bank—not the one that he had put the money in, and that we needed to go and find where the money had actually been put. I could not dissuade him. Finally, we got into the car and I followed his directions as to where to go. Down this street, down that one. Turn

Lucid

here. Turn there. After an hour of aimless driving, I convinced Mike that we should go home and try another day. After we got home, I was able to get the form that had upset him and hide it. Out of sight, out of mind—we did not have to go driving again.

Another problem solved. On to the next.

The tax forms came in the mail. Mike got them and clutched them in his hands. He was still holding them when I got home. He was fixated on getting the taxes done. Doing taxes had always been Mike's thing. Since the beginning of our marriage, Mike had spent every year from January to April going over the last year's expenses and making sure that everything balanced out to the last penny.

I found all the forms necessary for filing our taxes. It was no easy task. Mike had his papers strewn all over his study, spilling off his desk and off the card table he had set up to hold all the miscellaneous mail that came in. The junk mail had piled up for several years. He would not let me sort through it. Finally, in order to find what was needed to do the taxes as well as to get rid of my stress about the possible fire hazard, I started sneaking into the study while he his attention was focused on the TV and carrying out boxes of papers to the garage. There, I would sort through them and keep the one or two sheets that might be useful. I was glad that this strategy was working but also very saddened that Mike did not even realize what was going on. He did not notice the decline in his papers, and when I finally had the study all cleaned out, he never noticed that anything was different.

Finally, with all necessary documents in hand, I said that we would do taxes together. What a disaster! Mike couldn't understand that he could not do them by himself anymore. He could not understand that I was trying to help. In desperation, I snuck all the documents upstairs and did the taxes by myself. Mike never knew. I told him that the taxes were finished and that I had filed our taxes online. (It was the first time that I ever done taxes and the first time

No Sugar Added!

I had used TurboTax—who would have ever thought that hitting the send key on the computer could overwhelm a person with such a wave of relief?) Mike demanded to have the completed tax forms. I printed out the forms for him. He spent weeks trying to keep the forms in his hands. He would lose them, and I would have to print him another set. It was a very, very stressful time. And that is a huge understatement. He wanted to know how we were going to pay what we owed. I said I had paid online. For Mike, that was an incomprehensible statement.

After Mike was diagnosed, I realized that I had a small window of opportunity to get certain things done. I needed to get our wills in order, and I needed to make sure I had power of attorney. I visited a lawyer and explained our situation. He told me what I needed to do. I asked him to prepare the necessary documents.

With extreme cajoling, I managed to get Mike into the lawyer's office, and the lawyer went over all the documents. He then called in a couple of witnesses so that we could sign our wills and the power of attorney.

Mike crossed his arms over his chest, puffed out his checks, and said, "I am not signing anything."

I said, "That is fine. I am going to sign" and proceeded to sign. Then the lawyer said that he and the witnesses were going to step out of the room and make copies. As soon as they left, Mike asked me, "Why are we here? What are we doing?"

I replied, "You just need to write your name on the line that I will show you."

The lawyer and the witnesses came back in, and I told them, "Mike is ready to sign now." I took the documents, put them in front of Mike, told him where to sign, and he signed. And that was the last time Mike ever signed his name.

"Is what just happened really legal?" I asked the lawyer after everything was signed.

"There is a concept of temporary ability," he replied. "Now, if you had been married for only a few years and came in here with the same request and wanted to get power of attorney, then it would have been a different story. But you have been married for over forty years, and no one is trying to take advantage of anyone else, so I am comfortable with the situation."

We left, and I was so very relieved. I had power of attorney. As I was to find out over the next few years, power of attorney is a very powerful document. It made possible my taking care of Mike and taking care of our financial resources despite Mike's loss of the ability to sustain logical thought.

That evening, Mike asked me, "Why were we talking to that man today? What were we talking about?" I silently gave thanks for the legal concept of "temporary ability."

****

Mike had refused to roll over his 401(k) to an IRA when he retired. This was an early sign of Mike not processing things in a rational manner. Later, after he was diagnosed with vascular dementia and I was trying to make sure things were in order, I started to educate myself about 401(k)s, and I stumbled upon the concept of minimum required distributions (MRDs). I learned that you must take MRDs from certain retirement accounts after you reach the age seventy and a half or face stiff financial penalties. It was scary—Mike was approaching seventy, and I didn't know when to withdraw the money, or how much! I decided that we needed to talk to the person in charge of Mike's 401(k), so I made an appointment and drove us to downtown Houston for a discussion. I listened to what the financial advisor told Mike to do, listened to Mike's refusal to do anything and with an intense feeling of utter hopelessness, drove us back home.

No Sugar Added!

As soon as I obtained power of attorney, I contacted the financial institution again and set to work.

Kawai took Mike to the grocery store so that Shani could help me search Mike's study for the paperwork needed to roll over the 401(k). The good news was that Shani and I found the necessary paperwork. The not so good news was that Kawai could not stop Mike from filling the shopping cart with dog food, presumably intended for our dog Lycos, and packages of the vanilla crème filled cookies that Mike loved. She could not get him to put anything back. In order to not make a scene, she let him buy it all. She was in shock when the total came to $500. That was the last time we took Mike to the grocery store. I felt badly that that was the only solution we could come up with—short of bankruptcy—because Mike really seemed to enjoy shopping for pet food and his cookies.

But the good news was that I got Mike's 401(k) rolled over.

****

In June, four months after Mike's dementia diagnosis, he and I drove to our small cabin in New Mexico. Five years before, we had purchased the small isolated cabin, two bedrooms and a great deck, that backed up to the Santa Fe National Forest, with the thought that it would be an ideal place where the family could get together in the summer. We broke the trip in half and spent the night in San Marcos, Texas. We had a very pleasant time walking around after supper and talking about many things. I thought to myself, "Maybe I have been imagining the situations where Mike is fading from reality. Maybe things are really going to be OK." Only later did I realize that evening was to be our last "normal" evening.

The next day, as I was driving, Mike was attempting to read his Louis L'Amour book. Mike had read all of this author's great Westerns multiple times, and now he was trying to tell me what was

Lucid

on the page. My stomach dropped to my toes as I realized that he could no longer read. Losing the ability to read was sad beyond comprehension. Just two months before, he had finished reading *The Eruption of Khartoum.* He discussed it endlessly on the phone with Michael, our son, and encouraged him to read it. That was the last book that Mike ever read.

The second night, while we were at the cabin, Mike woke up and—in the deep darkness of the mountain night—he started screaming about skunks digging through the walls. His panicked descriptions had me almost convinced, and I was very relieved when I turned on the lights and did not see any rabid skunks with teeth bared, ready to attack. As soon as there was the first glimmer of morning light, I packed the car and we headed home. That was the last trip that just the two of us made to the cabin together. It was the beginning of our many years existing in realms of his increasingly fantastic confabulations.

Unlearning how to read and living in a world of major fabrications was a very bleak plateau indeed.

****

Because Kawai and Shani were stay-at-home moms and I was still working, they bore the brunt of these long years of confabulation.

While Mike could still use the phone, he started calling our daughters during the day, panicked, and imploring them to come over to check the house because someone was trying to break in or to come over because he wasn't ready for the president, who was landing in his helicopter behind the house. He told them stories of neighbors on the roof who were yelling at him, asking for help to come down. The scenarios were endlessly diverse, having in common only their length and convoluted bizarreness. The

No Sugar Added!

panicked requests became more frequent and increasingly fantastical as Mike's confabulations kicked into high gear. At every call, the girls would pack up their kids—Kawai with her two, and Shani with her three—and drive over to check on Mike. He needed them to drop everything and come over immediately. And they did.

When they arrived at the house, they would often find Mike in the backyard, standing in one place, arms straight up and extended to the sky, palms pointing heavenward, and chanting in an unknown tongue. Other times, he would be standing outside, head bowed, hands clasped in some type of meditative trance. Automatically, we started describing the days as an Indian Chief Day or a Buddha Monk Day.

One afternoon, Brinny was in the backyard, watching her grandpa. She remarked, "Grandpa is sure singing a lot this afternoon."

"Yes, and that is really funny because before your grandpa had dementia, he never sang," I replied.

"Well, I guess he can sing now because he has more room in his brain for songs, since he does not remember how to really talk right to us anymore!" she said.

The grandkids could always be counted on to contribute a unique perspective to the dementia experience!

****

I read about people who said that their loved one got sweeter and sweeter as they fell deeper and deeper into dementia. Unfortunately for us, Mike's caretakers, Mike instead got angrier and angrier. He lashed out at us verbally—and, as words started to fail him, physically. There was one huge exception to this behavior, and that was when our grandkids were around. Seeing him surrounded by his grandchildren, it was easy to forget that Mike

Lucid

was not his normal self. An impartial observer watching the interactions of Mike with his grandchildren would have concluded that Mike was just your run-of-the-mill grandpa. He even laughed with them!

For very short periods of time after his diagnosis, we even left Mike with the grandkids as the "responsible adult." But this practice ended abruptly one evening after Mike and I had had a very nice time taking all the grandkids out to Chick-fil-A. After supper, the kids all wanted to come over to our house to make sundaes. A sundae is not a sundae without a squirt of whipped cream on top. I knew there was no whipped cream at the house, so I figured that I would stop by the grocery store and quickly run in and get some. I parked in the parking lot. Everyone was belted in securely. I opened the window. Mike was happy, and he was an adult, so I knew I was not leaving the kids unattended in the van. I ran into the store and bought the whipped cream. As I hurried back out of the store, I heard a blaring alarm coming from our van. I saw a crowd of people in its vicinity, and heard someone yelling, "A man is trying to steal a van and kidnap all those kids! Call 911!"

I quickly thumbed the automatic car lock on the key fob, and all noise immediately ceased. The gathered crowd cheered and clapped. No one called 911. The shoppers continued going about their business. Looking into the van, I figured out what must have happened. Mike had decided to open more windows after I had left. He had leaned across the console to the driver's seat. Then he started pushing buttons, setting off the alarm. I opened the door and got into the van. The three youngest children were just sitting there, buckled in, contentedly sucking their pacifiers. Kate and Amberle were quite distraught and exclaimed to me, "Grandma, we thought you would never get back!" It was way past time to leave Mike alone with the kids—even only for a few minutes.

No Sugar Added!

****

Life became even more constrained. Mike could no longer be left at the homes of either of our daughters if I wanted to go out to dinner with friends. He would become very agitated and would refuse to stay in their houses. I would get a call in the middle of a pleasant dinner to come back and get him. I stopped going out unless someone could be at our house with Mike for the evening.

Mike and I went to our friends' home one evening for dinner. We had known them and been involved in Bible study groups with them for over twenty years. Mike sat with his arms folded, not responding to any of the hosts' attempts to get him to enter the conversation. The next day, Mike asked me, "Whose house were we at last night? Do we know those people?"

That was the last time we went out socializing together.

****

Scrambling to invent new ways of coping as Mike's mental function declined, was our way of life. Unfortunately, we never seemed to get ahead of the decrement curve!

For instance, I turned on the oven to warm it up before baking cookies. Underwear in the oven started a slow burn. Yes, Mike had put underwear in there.

Shani walked into the kitchen and saw a big hole in the ceiling where the overhead light fixture had been. Evidently, Mike had ripped it out. Of course, the electricity was still on, so Shani quickly tripped the circuit breakers until Jeff could come over and put in a new light fixture.

Underwear in the oven had an easy fix—check the oven before use. The removal of light fixtures had us stumped. We could not figure out how Mike had done it, because he had lost most of his fine motor control by then. For instance, he could not tie balloons for the kids and could no longer write his name legibly. (Interestingly, he was aware that he could not do these things but was totally unaware of the many other things he could not do.) So how did he manage to use the tools that were strewn about the kitchen? It was a mystery. All we could think of to do was to hide all tools and hope for the best. Fortunately, that worked, and no more electrical fixtures were ever ripped out.

****

As 2006 was drawing to a close, I started to think about Mike's approaching seventieth birthday.

Seventy seemed to be a milestone. I thought a surprise birthday party might be just the thing. I would invite everyone that Mike had been involved with over the years from church and in the neighborhood. It would be come and go. It was obvious that Mike was losing touch with the world that the rest of us lived in, and it would be good for Mike to spend time while he still could with everyone he had known over the years. Michael, our son, said, "Just tell me when, and I will fly home!" As it got closer to February 23, 2007, however, it became obvious that the idea was no longer feasible. The time for a surprise party was over. I had miscalculated. There was not enough of Mike still in this world for him to be part of celebrating turning seventy. Instead of the surprise party, I planned a family party where "gifts" were given to the grandchildren from their grandfather. After all, Mike would not really be aware of getting gifts, and it would be good for the grandchildren to have positive memories of their grandfather even if the gifts had not been chosen by him—his money did pay for them!

No Sugar Added!

We all agreed that Brooke, Mike's fifth grandchild, born on December 29, 2005 before Mike turned seventy in February of 2006, was the perfect birthday gift for Mike. Three years after being diagnosed with dementia, Mike was still capable of smiling while holding Brooke, and he was still capable of interacting with the other four granddaughters when they clambered into his lap—and, most importantly, he still knew their names. He was still three years away from being deemed "too scary" for the grandkids to approach him. At seventy, Mike had indeed been blessed by the Lord (even though he was not aware of it)!

****

The righteous will flourish like a palm tree
. . . .
They will bear fruit in old age.
—Psalms 92:12

OK, Lord. I get the concept of fruit in old age. But, really, LEMONS? Lord, we are making lemonade as fast as we can, but there is no sugar to add. We are drowning in the sour, undrinkable lemonade of old age!

Chapter 2

2007–2009: Scrambling

But as for me, I watch in hope for the Lord,
I wait for God my Savior,
My God will hear me.
-Micah 7:7

Mike's seventieth birthday had come and gone. Mike and I still lived in hope—well, at least I did, but I no longer hoped that we could have, and maintain, a meaningful relationship. My hope had morphed into a basic, no-frills-added hope that, with the family's help, we would be able to cope with whatever challenge the next cognitive drop presented. This hope included being able to care for Mike at home until the end.

By this time, we were presented with new challenges, both physical and emotional, on what seemed like a daily basis. Physical challenges generally lent themselves to some type of (admittedly inconvenient) physical response. But the emotional challenges generally only had one response—your soul being cut to the quick.

No Sugar Added!

For instance, one evening Mike dozed off where he was sitting and then suddenly jerked awake and yelled out to me, "Your father is upstairs. Go and get him. I have to talk to him."

"My father is dead," I said.

"Good God!" Mike exclaimed, very distressed. "When did that happen? No one ever told me!"

"Eleven years ago."

Mike started sobbing and howling with grief.

As quickly as I could, I got an ice cream cone out of the freezer and gave it to him. Busily consuming the ice cream, he forgot his grief. But I was unable to forget it myself, and I spent the rest of the evening crying and being haunted by the question, "When a person's memory is untethered and then a random, lost piece of forgotten memory of grief floats back to the surface, is that person condemned to going through the grieving process all over again?" I knew that no one would ever choose to experience such sadness.

One day, shortly after this sad evening, Mike started hollering to me to call some of his friends. Suddenly, he made the statement, "I have no friends!" How true. At this point, he did not.

"I have no friends!" This lament came from the deep sorrow of dementia. But Mike had family, and a family is much better than friends! After all, Psalm 68:6 says, *"God sets the lonely in families."* Who can be more utterly lonely than the demented? One can't be lonelier than the person who has lost even him or herself. I found comfort in changing that line in Psalms to read, *"God has set the demented in families,"* set them in families so that families retain and honor the memory of the demented, even as those families mutter under their breath, *"We do not know what to do, but our eyes are on you."* (2 Chron 20:12b)

But the psalmists have given the family a promise from God: *"Cast your cares on the Lord and he will sustain you."* (Psalm 55:22)

Lucid

Sustain you when Brooke says, "We need to love Grandpa even when his brain is broken." Sustain you when Amberle asks, "When will grandpa be normal again?" and she is using the word "normal" to mean the less demented state of two weeks before!

Gradually, there came the realization that one big challenge of dementia was that our family values—cultivated over more than forty years of marriage—were changing.

For instance, one important family value, which Mike and I had always agreed about, was the importance of sharing meals together. Shared meals gave us "enforced" times to talk together and make sure that we were on the same page. (Or, if it turned out—as many times it did—that we were not on the same page, at least we knew what page the other was on!) Even during the most hectic years, when we were both very involved with work and the activities of our three children, we as a family generally managed to eat at least one meal together.

When the children built lives of their own, Mike and I continued this tradition, but with the pleasant discovery that eating out was a great perk of living in an empty nest.

Then the evening came when Mike and I were eating at a local restaurant. For the first time in all the years that I knew him, he rejected his salad with verbal insults to the waiter and then aggressively argued with that waiter over the check. That was the last time I took Mike out to eat at a restaurant.

For a while, in an attempt to still preserve a semblance of mealtime together, Mike and I would "go out to eat" by me cajoling him into the van and then driving to the local Sonic Drive-In. Sitting there, I commented to Mike that it was just like old times—just like the summer before we were married. That summer, Mike and I would often drive to Sonic after work (we both worked at the Kerr-McGee Corporation in Oklahoma City, Oklahoma) and sit there in his burgundy Pontiac, windows rolled down, 1960s rock

No Sugar Added!

and roll blaring, dreaming together of our soon-to-be-shared future.

Later, when we were a young family with two preschoolers, our dining out preference continued to be Sonic. Now, I reminded Mike of our favorite Sonic memory—Shani telling us that what she knew what she wanted to be when she grew up: A Sonic employee, delivering food on roller skates. For years, we had laughed together about that.

Mike did not respond. Memories of those times were now gone. Reminiscing in the van at Sonic, I had come full circle. Mike had not. He was lost and wandering in a memory wasteland. For him, no event would ever again be "coming full circle."

Together, we should have been looking in the rearview mirror of life, rejoicing in dreams realized. Together, we should have been straining to peer into the future, speculating on what it held for our grandchildren.

Instead, we sat together but did not speak. I, alone, was holding all our shared memories. I alone was enjoying the gift of grandchildren bestowed upon us and the knowledge of the present.

The background rock and roll music was all that kept our meal from being eaten in silence.

All too soon, the time arrived when Mike tried to eat his hamburger without having removed the wrapper, and then soon after that he couldn't manage a hamburger at all. Our eating out days were finished. Cleaning up a food mess in the van was not worth the pleasure derived from "eating out."

One of the many sad, hard, and distressing aspects—actually, all aspects are very hard—of being the caretaker for someone with dementia is the necessity of robbing the person of their "free will," which is the Creator's gift to those he created in His image.

Mike and I had always tried to respect each other's individual preferences. Before we married, we had talked about how we would not try to change the other into our preferred personality. We had mostly succeeded against some large odds—think trying to keep oil and water in a non-separating emulsion! And then, because of dementia, and in an attempt to make my life more bearable, I gradually robbed Mike of this gift. Dementia tipped the scales in the favor of the caretaker. Having to be practical, I took away choice after choice from Mike. I actively enabled Mike's "tastes" to morph into mine. It just made things so much easier!

In the early stages of his dementia, Mike ate whatever was set before him with gusto. One day, Kawai saw him eating cabbage and said, "Mom, why are you feeding Dad cabbage? You know how much he hates cabbage, and he has never eaten it!"

"Well, he is eating it now, and he appears to be enjoying it!"

"I think it's morally wrong to give Dad food that you know he does not like. You remember what Dad doesn't like to eat—even if he doesn't!" she said.

"Well, he eats everything now," I told her. "For the first time in our marriage, my meal preparation does not have to take into consideration what Dad likes. He eats it all."

"That's just so wrong!"

Maybe Kawai was right about it being morally wrong to give Mike cabbage to eat, but the time had arrived when making life easier for the caretaker won out over any philosophical discussions about whether or not he should be given cabbage. During the next few years, this principle of practicality came into play again and again.

Mike was losing weight. Clothes were a problem. One afternoon, as he was standing in the backyard, his pants dropped to the ground. It was time to do something. I got him suspenders. He would not wear them. I could not take him to the store, so I went and bought pants, took them home, and had him try them on. If they were the wrong size, I returned them. By trial and error, he

No Sugar Added!

finally had pants that fit—for a while, until more weight was lost. A coworker provided me with the perfect answer. "He is generally not leaving the house, so just buy him lounging pants," she said. "The elastic waist will keep them up, and it will be easier for you to get him dressed."

Wearing lounge pants was no big deal, except that Mike had always worn a suit to work. Every day. When he no longer went into the office, he was generally dressed in what would be called business causal. I could not talk him into a "Houston summer casual look." Because a caretaker—me—was in charge of Mike's life and because this caretaker always went for easy solutions whenever possible, this preference of Mike's was also taken away. The person who refused to eat cabbage and always wore suits was no more. I realized that dropping from plateau to plateau could be defined by the loss of choices that make each of us an individual—such as me deciding that Mike could no longer choose to open the refrigerator.

Without supervision, Mike would go to the refrigerator and pull out food. He would take the food all over the house and scatter it. He would pour the milk out onto the floor. He would leave frozen items all over the place. This situation was solved by going to the internet and looking up refrigerator locks. Yes, there are such things! We bought two refrigerator locks from Amazon. We put one on the refrigerator door and one on the freezer door. Mike would go to the refrigerator door and shake it violently, but it would not open. When the door didn't open, he forgot that he wanted it opened and would walk away. Of course, it was a pain for the rest of us to have to find the key whenever we wanted to open the refrigerator or freezer, but finding the key was much better than mopping catsup off the wall!

Lucid

Soon after the lock was on the refrigerator, Mike had to be denied right of deciding when to go outside his house and even where he could walk around inside his own home.

Mike would go outside into the backyard. He would stand under the trees with hands clasped and chant meaningless syllables, which were punctuated with his hands raised to the sky as he bowed to the sun. It was a mesmerizingly bizarre scene to watch. He started leaving the backyard and pressing his face against the neighbors' back windows, peering in. Once he wandered into the next-door neighbor's front yard, and the wife came out onto her porch with a broom, shouting, "Shoo! Shoo!" It was time for action.

We put locks on all the doors. We also installed sensors on the outside doors that would sound an alarm if the door were opened. We put locks on all the gates in the backyard. The ringing of the front doorbell agitated Mike, so we disconnected it. My children and I laughed about our house being locked up tighter than Fort Knox—and it was.

Inside the house, we restricted Mike for his own safety. Instead of "babyproofing," we "dementia proofed." Everything was removed from the master bedroom, including the pictures that hung on the wall (which could be ripped off the wall and flung, breaking a window—or worse yet, flung and breaking a caretaker's head!) except for the bed and a couple of cheap, comfortable recliners, which were of course not fabric covered! The fake leather covering was a little slippery, so Mike would sometimes slide off onto the floor. We put Velcro strips on the seat to make it a little rougher and hoped that the strips would snag his lounge pants and make it a little harder for him to slide off. And that worked, to a degree. I reversed the door handle so that it locked from the outside, not the inside. That way, when Mike was really agitated, he could be kept in the bedroom until he had calmed down. I put stacked baby gates (stacked because I was afraid that a single baby gate could cause Mike to trip and fall if he tried to step over it) across the door that went from the bathroom to the bedroom so that Mike could not go into the bathroom, turn on the water, and flood the floor—which had happened.

****

Hurricane evacuation presented us with a great opportunity to exercise a little creativity in dementia problem-solving. Unfortunately, we did not pass this test with flying colors, but we did pass. (Our bar for passing was very low. By this time on our dementia journey, we counted just surviving as a passing grade on any dementia test we were given).

Hurricane Ike was in the Gulf of Mexico and heading straight for Houston. Our area was ordered to evacuate. Kawai was in the hospital, having just given birth to our sixth grandchild, Caleb. She and day-old Caleb evacuated directly from the hospital along with the rest of her family. Mike and I and our dog, Lycos, were in our van and Shani and her family were in their van. Shani had a friend in Austin who offered to let us stay in their empty rental house. So we headed out in a three-van caravan to Austin.

We made it. A strange house, a new baby, the coming and going of people, and the constant TV weather watch drove Mike into a frenzy of bizarre confusion. Somehow, he had latched onto a pair of sunglasses and would not take them off. He marched around the rental house, chanting. He would not sit. He would not sleep. Every time Kawai woke in the night to feed Caleb, she would see her father march by wearing one less piece of clothing than the time before until she saw him march by totally nude. She said it was like living in a nightmarish zombie movie. (I slept through the whole night, totally unaware.) Living as evacuees was so stressful that as soon as Ike cleared Houston, I loaded Mike up in the van and we headed home. I could not even wait for the all clear before going back. I figured that no matter what we found when we got home, it would be an improvement over being refugees. And it was. No electricity and a yard full of limbs, leaves, and uprooted trees did not bother Mike. Somehow, Mike knew that he was back home, and he immediately flipped into his "normal" demented state—no sunglasses and clothes staying on as soon as we entered our house.

From Ike onward until the end of our dementia journey, we as a family had one recurring conversation, which started with the question, "What will we do if we have to evacuate again?" The only answer I ever came up with was, "I will just remain at home with Dad and if we are blown away, at least he and I will be blown away together." No family member appreciated my defeatist attitude, they thought I was just giving up, but then again, no one had anything better to offer. Fortunately for us, for the rest of Mike's life all summers after Ike were free of hurricanes in the Gulf of Mexico.

****

As a novice traveling down Dementia Road, I was totally blindsided by where Mike and I ended up. Never in a thousand years would I have thought that in our final years together we would not be members of a local church.

The biggest decision Mike and I made before our marriage was to always attend the same church, worshiping together. We realized that this decision would require some compromises from both of us because we each had strong beliefs, and what we each believed differed on some points—but going to church together was always a top priority.

We agreed that the primary value we wanted to give any children we might be blessed with was *"to love the Lord your God with all*

No Sugar Added!

your heart, and all your mind and all your soul. And to love your neighbor as yourself." One way we would show this love would be by worshiping and serving God together as part of a local church congregation. And so we did.

And then, going to church started to become a problem.

Ever since resigning from the mission committee, Mike had lost all sense of belonging. Every Sunday morning, I brought him to his Adult Bible Study class and then went and taught my Sunday School class of fourth graders. As soon as his class was finished, he would come and stand at my door. No one talked to him. I did not blame anyone for not wanting to talk with him. Conversations with Mike were hard and mostly bizarre. Your question about today's weather would either be ignored completely or answered with a strange confabulation about having to be careful when the president came through the door. He would follow me into the main service. We sat there. Mike would watch me and do whatever I did. When I stood, he stood. When I bowed my head, he bowed his head. I would sit there, keeping watch over Mike. If he started to stand at the wrong time, I would give him a gentle push with my hand that kept him seated. At the conclusion of the service, he would follow me out—always two steps behind. (I could never figure out why, no matter when or where we were walking together, Mike would always follow two steps behind me. He never would walk with me side by side.) While driving us home, I would ask, "What happened in your Sunday school class this morning? Who was there? What was the lesson about?" Mike did not answer the questions with words but only with a slow, negative shaking of his head and a stream of tears.

It was time to do something different on Sunday. But what? I still wanted to go to church. I still wanted Mike to go to church.

Hurricane Ike was the catalyst for change.

Lucid

For the first few Sundays after we returned home from our hurricane evacuation, road conditions in Houston were such that we could not drive to the church where we had been parishioners for over twenty years. However, only five minutes from our house was a church that our daughters and their families attended. I decided to try going there. I still wanted both Mike and me to participate in something together for the Lord. I thought that the grandkids seeing their grandparents sitting together in church every Sunday would show them that worshipping God was still an important part of our lives. This was my way of following the instructions of 1 Timothy 5:4, *"But if a widow has children or grandchildren, these should learn first of all to put their religion into practice by caring for their own family and praying for their parents and grandparents, for this is pleasing to God."*

After about six months of not attending the church where we had been members for over twenty years, we received a letter in the mail saying that we were no longer members, since we had not been there for six months. Never once had anyone from the church called to ask where we were. Various members of the congregation and the staff of the church knew of Mike's diagnosis of vascular dementia. No one ever called to ask how he was doing or how the caretaking was going.

An interesting side note: One Sunday, as Mike and I sat together in church, listening to the pastoral prayer, I was struck with the realization that every single Sunday people with just about every condition—the cancer victims, the heart victims, the destitute, the depressed—were prayed for, but never once was there ever a prayer for the demented to be comforted, or for the caretakers of the demented to be given the strength to get through one more day.

That is how, after over forty years of us being members together of local churches, Mike and I were now nonmembers together. But

No Sugar Added!

no matter—Mike and I were still members of the Body of Christ, still God's children, and still members of the Kingdom of God.

And of course, members or not, we continued going to church every Sunday—even if it was not to the church where we had worshipped before for so many years.

Every Sunday, I got up and started to get Mike ready for church. He did not shave himself—although at that point, he still could've if he would've! So, on Saturday night, I shaved him. Generally, it was a battle. I would have to get him close to his chair and then, with a not-so-gentle shove, push him to a seated position. Then, with one hand, I would shave him while the other hand kept him in the chair. It was not a "barbershop quartet" idyllic moment. Mike would be screaming, "Help! Help! She is killing me! Come help me!" and I would be loudly commanding, "Just sit still!" (It had to be loud so that I could be heard over the shouting.) I felt justified. After all, we were getting ready to worship the Lord, and it was the one time every week that Mike got to be out of the house.

I had to get him into pants, tightly cinching the belt so that they would not fall. He always put his jacket on willingly. There seemed to be some lingering memory that this is what he did. He had worn a jacket to work for over forty years, so the reflexive movement of donning a jacket was automatic.

The getting-ready-for-church process had to start early on Sunday morning because it was always an adventure to get Mike suitably attired. After getting Mike dressed, I faced the tricky part: I had to entice Mike into the car. Task accomplished; we could finally drive to church.

When we arrived at the church, Mike would get out of the car and follow me, two steps behind, into the sanctuary. It was not an easy task to get to our seats, and I could not let him get separated from me. The church exuded Southern Baptist friendliness and hospitality. There was a gauntlet of folks waiting to shake hands

Lucid

and welcome us to the service. I held my breath, never knowing what bizarre behavior a friendly welcome would set off in Mike. We just needed to get in and find seats. We got there early so that I could, without "welcoming" distractions, get Mike up (of course following two steps behind me) to a secluded balcony spot.

I relaxed slightly when I got Mike seated with our daughters' families surrounding us. I felt good, knowing that if Mike started behaving inappropriately, there were two strong sons-in-law there who could help me handle him and maybe get him out with a minimal disturbance. But when he was surrounded by family, his actions were always appropriate. He stood when we all stood, and he sat when we all sat. You can't ask for much more than that. He even would open his mouth and utter nonsensical phrases during the congregational singing. Maybe it was only my wishful thinking, but Mike always did seem to be sort of at peace during the service.

In one of the many articles I read on the internet about dementia, there was one about memory-cueing in the demented—how things from the past can bring forth emotional responses. So, it made sense that a lifelong experience of worship, for instance, appeared to cue an appropriate worship response.

It did not seem too farfetched to me, watching Mike in church, to think that maybe this was also part of what the admonition of *"train up a child in the way he should go and when he is old, he will not depart from it"* meant. In other words, what has been cued stays cued almost forever.

At the closing prayer, I was primed and ready to make our rapid exit to the car. Safely in the van, I always breathed a slow sigh of relief and uttered a short prayer: "Thank you, God, for letting us worship in church for one more Sunday."

The last Easter that Mike went to church started with him dressed in his heavy-hooded, black winter jacket. When I told him that I was dressing him for church, so he needed to take it off, he

No Sugar Added!

replied that he was wearing his robe to introduce me to the father, the mother, and his fourteen other wives. This started me thinking about the connection between dementia and Easter.

It was so hard for all of us to watch Mike turn into a totally different person from the one that we had all known. Interacting with Mike now, it was hard to remember who he had once been. It was hard to remember that here was someone who grew up in absolute poverty but had had a dream that originated somewhere inside of him to go to college. He worked hard and paid for every hour of college himself. It was hard to remember how much his family meant to him and how much pleasure each of his children gave him. Mike was our children's patient parent. When the children were very young, he was the parent that got up with them in the night. Mike was the parent who helped with the math homework. I will always remember once when I was traveling for work, calling home in the evening to see how things were going. Mike answered the phone and said, "I don't have time to talk to you tonight. I have too much math homework to get explained." Mike went to innumerable band concerts and marching band contests to support his daughters. Mike stepped up and offered to be the coach of Michael's various basketball teams when there would have been no team because there ws no coach. The first time he volunteered to coach basketball I said, "You have never played on a team. What do you know about coaching basketball?" Mike replied, "True, I never had the opportunity to play but I did grow up in Indiana."

When Michael became involved with Future Farmers of America, Mike willing traveled even further out of his comfort zone. I will always remember coming home from work and finding Mike still dressed in his work suit and tie, kneeling on the kitchen floor helping blow dry the three chickens that Michael had just bathed in order to get them ready for the big FFA auction that evening. And just in case you are wondering, bathing chickens in the kitchen creates quite a mess.

To know Mike now, you would never guess at what kind of man he had been. The negative delta (previous self, minus present self) was just too large. And it was hard to think about this negative delta in general—it was just too sad and scary because it made me realize that we are all just a few broken blood vessels away from the same delta.

So how does Easter figure into this?

Easter is a time when we focus on the resurrection of Jesus and think about Him walking out of the tomb transformed. We think about this being the promise that one day we, too, will be transformed. This positive delta between what we are now and what we shall be is beyond anything that we can comprehend. But by observing and thinking about the negative delta seen in dementia, we can appreciate and more fully anticipate the positive delta that we will all experience in the future.

And that was what the fifteenth wife thought about that Easter Sunday.

And then there was a Sunday in late October when I "knew" that our churchgoing days were over. It was time for Mike to not go anymore. There was nothing specific that happened that made me know it, but I knew.

From then on, I went by myself. And no, it was not more restful. I left Mike at home. I could leave Mike home alone for short periods of time because of the video cameras that Jeff had installed around the house. I left the house with the doors unlocked—after all, you can't leave someone locked in a house if they don't know how to unlock doors—but I watched both him and the doors on my cell phone during the service. Only rarely did I have to leave the service early because I saw that Mike was on the move. I went into church quickly and left just as quickly. There was no time for idle chitchat. As I hurried home, it was always with a prayer of thanksgiving that once again God had been gracious and allowed me to worship Him with others in a community of faith.

Church was Mike's last tenuous connection to the world. And then it, too, was broken.

Chapter 3

2009-2012: Surviving, but Just Barely

May the favor of the Lord our God rest upon us—
Yes, establish the work of our hands.
—Psalm 90:17

On the afternoon of Sunday, May 11, 2009, I was upstairs sleeping. For the next several weeks, I would be sleeping during the day because I would be supporting, in Mission Control, the third shift of the last Hubble Space Telescope repair mission. After I had been asleep for a couple of hours, Shani came into the house, yelling for me to wake up and go take care of Dad. She had just driven up to the house and found an ambulance in the driveway, Mike sitting in a chair in the neighbor's living room, and many of the neighbors congregated in our front yard. I quickly ran over. The paramedics questioned me and then said that Mike

No Sugar Added!

appeared to be all right. His blood pressure and heart rate were good. Evidently, while I was sleeping, he had gotten out of the house and was standing in the driveway when the next-door neighbor saw him and asked how he was doing—a nice, neighborly, friendly question. Mike had replied that he thought he was having a heart attack. He then said that he did not know where I was, but he thought I was gone and never coming home again. The neighbor then did what a neighbor should do. He took Mike into his house and called 911, and the ambulance came.

After the ambulance left, Shani and I got Mike back into his own house, and the neighbors went back to their normal, Sunday afternoon activities.

There were locks on all the doors and video cameras already in place, we now made sure that the locks were always locked, no exceptions. (I had been a little cavalier about keeping all doors locked when I was home, while constantly running in and out the house.) In addition, Kawai and Shani's computers at home and their phones were connected to the video cameras so that they also could be aware of where Mike was. I would inform them when I was going to sleep during the day so that they would know when to be sure to be watching.

Par for the course of this family's dementia journey, this "ambulance adventure" was just another example of how we always seemed to lag one step behind the fluid, ever-changing circumstances involving Mike. These simple decisions should have already been made. There had been clues.

There was the day when Shani showed up at the house and Mike was nowhere to be found. She called me at work, and I said I'd rush home to help in the search. She then started to drive up and down the streets to see if she could find him.

Shani pulled up into the driveway just as I pulled in. Mike was sitting in her front seat, grinning. As I hurried to the van to get

Lucid

three-year-old Brooke out of her car seat, she threw up her arms and exclaimed, "Grandma, we have had a great adventure! We have been on a grandpa hunt, and we found him!" An adventure, indeed. After this "grandpa hunt," my daughters and I decided not to ever leave Mike home alone. We just never knew that we needed a checklist to make sure that all doors were locked, and all security precautions were in place before I went to sleep.

We were staying 24/7 with Mike, but still fudging that a teensy, weensy little bit. The girls divided the time while I was at work. When I worked the midnight to eight shifts, it was a little harder because it meant that someone had to sleep at the house and then hurry home to get the kids off to school because their spouses, who had spent the night with the kids, had to go to work. On these days, Mike was left at home alone for no more than thirty minutes. We all felt comfortable with that. I mean, what could happen in less than thirty minutes? One morning about a month after the ambulance incident, I walked into the house at eight in the morning. Kawai, who had spent the night, had already left to get her kids ready for school. When I walked into the house, I found Mike sitting on the couch in the den with two female strangers, who were examining his leg. The strangers looked up when I came in and told me that they had been walking by, and Mike had hollered to them that his leg was broken, and would they please come in and help him? They had come in. They were looking a little puzzled because Mike did not seem to be in any pain at all, no matter where they touched his leg. I went through the dementia explanation, thanked them profusely for being such kind neighbors, and hurriedly shepherded them back out the front door.

Because of Kawai's and Shani's willingness to stay with Mike while I worked, I had been able to continue working during the first years of Mike's dementia. I was even able to continue to do the travel required by my job. The girls just split the time I was gone. I used Mike's pension to pay them. They insisted that there was no need to pay them—after all, Mike was their father—but as I explained to them, I was working to maintain my sanity. Mike and I could get along nicely without his pension. I jokingly said to the girls, "You have it all. You both wanted to be stay-at-home moms—and here you are staying with your kids all day long while you are here watching grandpa and getting paid for it!" Their immediate reply was, "But we wanted to be stay-at-home moms in our own houses, not in our parents' house!"

Susan Jacoby wrote in her book *Never Say Die*, "Ideally, we would all have someone who loves us enough to accompany us through the valley of the shadow. In the real world, many people are denied this ultimate grace."

We, Mike's family, provided this ultimate grace for Mike.

The wisdom of this decision was confirmed shortly after lunch one Sunday during this time. Mike suddenly started to cry. Very loudly, he asked, in a broken voice, "But what will become of me?"

Startled, I answered, "You are here and will continue to be here, in your own house, being taken care of by those who love you."

"Thank you," Mike responded. The crying stopped, the repetitive pacing started again, and the Hallmark moment was over—never to be remembered by Mike, but always to be remembered by me.

After I related this incident to Kawai and Shani, Kawai said, "One of the saddest things about dementia is that it makes you think about 'me, the caregiver' instead of the afflicted, like, 'How hard this is for me? How hard it is to be a caretaker!' These feelings are just so self-centered. I hate that I have them!"

****

Lucid

Caleb was one. Mike was seventy-two. At the same time, Mike and Caleb both started to become obsessed with sweeping. Mike always had a broom in hand, sweeping, and the swoosh, swoosh, swooshing sound of the broom continually filled the house. Caleb, who was just learning to walk, was fascinated with brooms. In the kitchen, he would grab the broom, generally propped against the wall, and try to sweep. Seeing Caleb with a broom, Mike would yank it away from him. Caleb would cry. Mike would furiously sweep. To stop the escalating Broom Wars, I bought more brooms. There were brooms everywhere in the house. But there were not enough for Mike to let Caleb have one of his own. I wrote names on the brooms—Mike on some, Caleb on the others. When Mike grabbed Caleb's broom, I pointed to the name and said, "See, this broom is Caleb's. His name on it proves it!" Of course, I knew at the time that putting names on brooms was a totally futile gesture, because Mike was way past reading and understanding names, but I did it anyway. Rational thought does not always rule a caretaker!

The Broom Wars were a perfect example of the parabola of life. Image a life that was graphed with a y-axis of acquisition of new skills and an x-axis of zero to 100 percent of a lifetime. At birth a baby is at point 0, 0 and rapidly ascends the x-y slope. This upward climb on the left side of the parabola continues for years and then plateaus off somewhere in mature adulthood. Ideally, a person would remain steadily on the top of the plateau until he or she dies. But old age pushes most of us down the right-hand side of the parabola as we start to lose more and more skills. The Broom Wars were a perfect illustration of the ascending and descending sides of the parabola of life. Caleb and Mike were at the exact same point on the y-axis, but on opposite sides of the x-axis. Caleb was ascending rapidly, and Mike was descending just as rapidly, but for a short moment in time they were at the very same point—fighting over brooms.

No Sugar Added!

Caleb rapidly outgrew his broom fascination and moved on to acquiring new skills. Mike continued his sweeping until he descended to where he could no longer hold the broom.

****

Since almost right after his dementia diagnosis, Mike had not slept through the night. Very early in the dementia process, he lost all concept of day and night. When the sun started to set, Mike's agitation ramped up exponentially. This common aspect of demented behavior is very aptly named sundowning, or sundown syndrome. I tried giving Mike melatonin, to see if that would help, but it made no difference.

He did not know how to go to bed—this was a very interesting but also a very aggravating phenomenon. For years after his diagnosis, Mike appeared not to have even a trace of circadian rhythm. He slept when he slept, unconnected to any daily activities. When he was awake, he constantly paced around the house, but when he was sleeping, he could sleep anywhere—such as in his chair.

When the dark of night no longer impeded Mike's incessant roaming over the entire house, for my safety and for Mike's safety, he had to be confined to our bedroom while I slept. Two baby gates, the kind that screwed into the doorframe, were stacked in the doorway, one on top of the other. In order to be available when Mike needed me, I slept on an inflatable mattress in the room just the other side of the gates. This ensured that I would hear him if he yelled, "Help!" or if he sank to the floor. (For me, there would be no more sleeping on a bed for the next five years.)

One evening, as I was situating us for the night—me to sleep, Mike to roam—the following poem popped into my head fully formed, as I raced around to find the wipes after being "surprised

Lucid

by feces" as I was changing Mike's Depend adult diaper while I was getting him ready for "bed."

Life

When I was young
Seeking employment
I flew planes
Always aware of the location of a suitable landing field
If needed for an emergency landing.

Now I am old
Seeking unemployment
From 24/7 caretaking
Always aware of the location of wet wipe packets
If needed for fecal containment.

(I immediately emailed this poem to my children, expecting replies of admiration for my latent literacy skills, which had clearly been enhanced by dementia caretaking. The only reply I received was from Kawai, the English major, who said, "You think this is poetry? Maybe dementia is catching, and this is the first symptom of it that you are exhibiting. :)"

I replied, "I loved my poem—and after all, how many poems have you ever read that encapsulated an entire life in two short stanzas?"

Sometimes the sound of urine hitting the bedroom floor would wake me up. Other times, if I had forgotten to take the broom out of his room, the rhythmic swoosh, swoosh, swooshing sounds would wake me up. Checking on Mike, I would see him there in the dimness of the nightlight, sweep, sweep, sweeping. The darkness of the night compounded the sadness of it all.

First thing one morning, while it was still dark, I went into the bedroom. Mike was standing there, drenched in urine.

"Good morning. How are you today?" I asked.

With a loud sob, Mike replied, "I am nothing!"

I immediately said, "You are Mike Lucid—child of God, wonderful husband, wonderful father, and wonderful grandfather."

By the time I had finished, Mike had stopped sobbing and had slid down onto the recliner in a stupor.

Although Mike had immediately forgotten the incident, it stayed with me all day long with great sadness.

*****

Mike continued to decrement. We coined the term termed "Magpie Ops" to describe the next phase.

As Mike paced around the house, he collected things—pins, medals, old cufflinks, and scraps of paper, and he tucked all these collectibles here and there.

Then he would sit for extended periods of time at the table, moving his Magpie Collection around and lifting, turning, and studying each object. Occasionally he would make sounds that we interpreted as laughter. We liked to think that Mike was contented and happy with his collection.

Finally, Mike stopped his constant, all-day-long pacing. He no longer swept compulsively and continuously. Instead, for long stretches of time, he would sit in the same chair and constantly fold towels. This was certainly more restful to be around than the pacing, so we left a laundry basket of clean towels next to his chair so that he would always have towels to fold.

Lucid

Mike no longer remembered how to eat. When we gave him his meals, we had to watch him eat, in order to make sure that he did. Otherwise, food would be found on windowsills or on top of the piano. Also, Mike no longer remembered how to take a shower. He forgot what he was doing between starting to shower and finishing.

Mike often missed the toilet when he urinated. Many times, he did not even try for the toilet. In order to protect the furniture against his wet clothing, I searched the internet and bought him different types of padded underwear. They were a waste of money, because we did not find a brand that really contained the urine.

Mike tended to sit in the same chairs in the den, so we tried putting washable pads on them for protection. Mike just threw the pads on the floor. We sewed slipcovers for the chair cushions and put the washable pads in them. And that worked. We had to remove the covers and the pads to wash them, but the cushions stayed dry.

Mike talked very little, and when he did, we generally couldn't understand what he said.

One day, our son Michael called. I talked to him for a long time and then gave the phone to Mike so that he could talk. As I listened to Mike's end of the conversation, it made no sense. Abruptly, Mike hung up—no goodbyes—and then he started sobbing, saying, "I don't even know how to talk to my own son anymore."

It was just too sad. I quickly got Mike a bowl of ice cream—Kawai's answer to her dad's sobbing—and gave it to him, and he was happy. He forgot that he couldn't talk to his son on the phone. He did not realize that he would never again talk to his son on the phone. But I knew, and all I could do was just to follow the instruction in the Psalms to *"be still before the Lord and wait patiently for Him."*

No Sugar Added!

One afternoon, after Mike had sat in a stupor for hours in his chair, all of a sudden, he blurted out the question, "Do you love me?"

I answered, "Yes, of course! Don't I watch you all the time and provide for your every need?" It was a regular Fiddler on the Roof moment, except that I did not break out in song.

Mike and I had one more lucid conversation during this time. I undressed Mike and tucked him into bed. As usual, I said, "Good night. I love you."

Then Mike asked, "Do I love you?"

I answered, "Yes."

Mike sighed with relief and said, "Good night. I love you, too, whoever you are."

This was the last "rational" conversation that Mike and I ever had.

****

One night, when I checked on Mike before going to sleep, he was sitting in his room—so sad, so dejected and sobbing, and saying over and over, "Memories, memories—I need memories." I could not give him memories, but I could give him an ice cream cone.

But really, we all need our memories, not ice cream. Having memories is a basic human need.

Without our memories and without remembering our past, we lose not only our yesterdays but also our todays and our tomorrows. Dementia is not just about losing your past. It is also about losing your moorings in the present.

As the biblical young David prepared to march out against the giant Goliath, he remembered his past. Remembering was part of his preparation. He said to those who doubted his ability to slay a giant, *"The Lord who delivered me from the paw of the lion and the paw of the bear, will deliver me from the hand of the Philistines."* (1 Sam 17:37) David's confidence in achieving victory today was rooted in remembrance of victories of yesterday.

When people no longer remember the ways in which their God has loved and provided for them throughout their lives, what hope do they have for God's love and provisions for today and tomorrow? What can rescue the demented person from such hopeless desolation and despair?

****

Once again, summer rolled around. Mike continued to become more and more difficult to take anywhere. The girls, the grandkids, and I wanted to take our annual summer trip to the cabin. We remembered the summer when the girls, the grandkids, and I made our annual trip to the cabin without Mike—but of course, Mike was not left alone in Houston in our absence. From the time of his diagnosis, Mike had never been left alone in Houston. There was always a family member close by to check on him. And that summer, Jeff was not going to the cabin because of his workload—therefore, he was the designated "Mike checker."

On our way back home, we stopped to spend the night in Childress, Texas. While in Walmart picking up Lunchables for the kids' suppers, I called Mike to check up on him and to inform him where we were, because I knew that he would not remember. He asked where I was and didn't understand my perky answer. He said, "I just feel so alone, and I don't know where I am." I immediately called Jeff and asked that he go over and spend the night at our house. He did. Mike was never left overnight alone in the house again.

No Sugar Added!

The next summer when it came cabin time, Mike had to go with us, since he could not be left home alone. And yes, we had to go. Traditions were not meant to be broken!

I perused the internet for advice. All the advice I gleaned from scouring the internet about traveling with a demented person was summarized by three words: DON'T DO IT! That advice was hard to accept, so we decided to maximize our chances for successful travel. Surely, we were smart enough and creative enough to make it work!

If someone had challenged our decision to ignore the DON'T DO IT! advice, we would have had to admit that at the last of Kate's softball games that we took Mike to, we experienced a vivid foreshadowing of travel difficulties with Mike.

Mike had become more and more difficult to take places. Generally, I could take him to the granddaughters' softball games, and he would sit quietly in his lawn chair. But at the last game, he had gotten up and started to walk away. I stood up and attempted to guide him back to his lawn chair. He shook my hand off his arm and kept on marching. He made it to the road that looped through the park. He would not listen to me or the girls, who were asking him to turn around. He kept on marching. I marched alongside him. Shani got into the van and trailed us. Our plan was to get Mike corralled and then slowly close in on him until he entered the van. However, our plans were not Mike's plans.

Mike got to the park entrance and started to walk onto Bay Area Boulevard, a very busy street. I got in front of him. Shani blocked him from the rear with the van. Kawai got on the other side. He would not let anyone near him. Kawai opened the passenger door. The closer any of us got to Mike, the more he backed away. It was like trying to coax an escaped wild buffalo back into its enclosure. We moved in closer, inching him toward the van. Finally, Mike grabbed the handle of the opened van door. We rapidly closed in.

Lucid

    I gently pushed him down onto the seat, lifted his legs, and swung him into the car—being hit only twice by his battling fists. I drove him home, missing Kate's home run. And that was the saga of Mike's last softball game.

    Again, just to be crystal clear, on a rational level we all understood the DON'T DO IT! warning. But our rational thinking could not overrule our emotions. We wanted to go! After all, we were, experienced, creative problem solvers. We could do it!

    We decided to take two vans and drive, bringing Mike with us. We left early on Sunday morning. We hadn't gotten out of Houston yet when Kawai, who was driving in van number two with Mike and Caleb, called Shani, who was driving van number one, and said, "We have to pull over. Dad is screaming about his legs hurting, and he is trying to escape from the van."

    We pulled over. Not wanting to disappoint the kids, we, right there in a Wendy's parking lot, transferred our luggage from Kawai's vehicle to Shani's. Kawai turned around and went back home with Mike and Caleb while the rest of us continued driving down the interstate. That evening in Amarillo, as the kids luxuriated in our hotel suite, I ordered Kawai her first Kindle to make me feel not quite so badly that she was at home with Mike, and we were on the road without her. And already I was trying to figure out a better and much-improved plan to make it possible for Mike to come with us the next summer. I had decided that the phrase DON'T DO IT! could not rule our lives.

    What hubris!

    The next summer, still not willing to surrender to DON'T DO IT! we headed to the cabin, implementing our new and improved dementia travel plan. I got Mike a pain medication prescription for leg cramps. I figured that we could give it to him just before he got in the car, and that would keep his legs from cramping. We would have him sit in the middle row in the van and maximize his

No Sugar Added!

legroom. We would stop at rest areas with family restrooms so that I could go into the restroom with him. (We had stopped letting Mike go into the men's restroom unaccompanied after having to go in and get him when he could not find his way out.)

We made it almost to the cabin without incident. At the very end, just as we started to congratulate ourselves on our great abilities to cope with dementia and our planning skills, and just as we started driving up a twisty, winding mountain road, Mike suddenly grabbed an unopened can of Pepsi and flung it at a grandchild's head. Fortunately, it missed both the child's head and all the windows. After that, we made sure that Mike could reach nothing but soft pillows!

After a week at the cabin, it was time to head home again. After a long day of driving, we stopped at a Best Western for the night. We got two rooms—Mike and I in one and the girls and all the kids in the other. Before going to sleep, I made sure the door was locked and had piled furniture in front of it so that if Mike tried to get out of the room during the night, I would hear the furniture falling.

I fell sound asleep. In the middle of the night, I was woken when I heard that Mike was up and saw a light on in the bathroom, but it was the smell that really yanked me out of my deep sleep.

I flipped on the light and saw Mike standing close to the bathroom door, looking totally lost and bewildered, with feces running down his legs. Feces was on the floor. Feces was on the tub. Feces was on the wall. The smell was overpowering. I started to croon, "It's OK, Mike, it's just OK. I will clean you up and put you to bed again."

Frankly, I did not know where to start. As usual in life—if you don't know where to start, just start where you are. So that's what I did. Leaving Mike standing in the bathroom doorway, I gingerly tiptoed to the tub. I reached for a towel, turned on the tub faucets, got the towel wet, and started to wipe up the floor and then rinse

Lucid

the towel in the tub. Wipe and rinse, wipe and rinse. When there was a "clear" path to Mike, I started to wipe him up. I put the toilet lid down and got him to sit on it. I got another towel and got it wet with warm water. I started to wash Mike's feet. At that moment, the scene of Jesus washing the disciples' feet just before the Last Supper popped into my head. Immediately, there amid the dripping brown towels, the smell, the brown feet, I felt the overwhelming presence of the Lord. I was at peace. And then out loud I said, "Thank you, Lord, for loving Mike and me. Thank you for caring for us. Thank you for the privilege of being able to make Mike clean." I know, it sounds crazy, but this was one of the most profound worship experiences I have ever had.

Finally, Mike was clean and tucked back into bed. Then I worked on getting the towels clean so that the next morning, when someone came to clean the room, they would not find a mess that would ruin anyone's day.

Morning came, and we were back on the road—a two-van caravan with Shani, me, and the kids in the lead and Kawai and Mike following. After a couple of hours, I saw in the rearview mirror that Kawai had pulled over to the side of the road. I called her and asked what the problem was. She said, "I had to pull over. Somehow, Dad got the door open and is now trying to unbuckle his seat belt and get out. I guess I forgot to have the child locks in place." She got the door closed with Mike still belted in, and once again we were on the road.

The last gas stop just about did us in. I took Mike to the bathroom, we put gas in the car, and then tried to get Mike into the van. He was not going. He pushed us away and would not let us get close to him. He tried to get away from us. The three of us adults encircled him (the kids were seat belted in the van) and tried to maneuver him into the vehicle. With his eyes blazing with fear, Mike tried to push us out of the way. So, there we were, four adults doing some kind of crazy ballet, weaving around gas pumps and cars that were moving by. Maybe one of the most bizarre things was that all around us, cars were being filled with gas and windshields were being wiped, but absolutely no one seemed to notice our dance. Finally, Shani enticed Mike into his seat with the ever-magical ice cream cone.

Once again, our two-van convey was on the road, with plans to not stop until we were in the driveway at our home. Together, we vowed to never travel with Mike again. The three of us were in firm agreement. There comes a point—which we were well past—when you should not try to travel with a demented person.

We grudgingly conceded defeat to DON'T DO IT!

****

Another school year started. The grandkids were a little older and involved in more activities. It was getting harder and harder for the girls to split their time to stay with Mike. We decided to try to hire someone to stay with him.

I asked around to see if any of my friends knew of someone that they would recommend. Several had women who had been doing childcare for them. Because my friends' children were getting older, they no longer needed childcare help and wanted to find work for their employees. I talked to several who were eager to work, and I had them stay with Mike. They did not understand dementia and, after spending a few hours alone with Mike, did not want the job. Mike was just too scary for them.

We all understood Mike being "scary." Just before Halloween, Kate's class in middle school had been instructed to list six of the scariest things they could think of to use for writing prompts. Her grandfather made the list.

Lucid

During the great caretaker hunt, I thought about the countless sermons based on Jesus's parable of the Good Samaritan I had heard over the years. But had I ever heard a sermon based on the bit player in the story—the innkeeper, i.e., the caretaker. There certainly should be sermons about the caretaker, because the odds are that most of us will end up taking care of someone else at one time or another! I thought—many times, really—that the Good Samaritan had it easy. He just loaded that injured stranger up on the donkey and then dumped him off with a bag of money at the innkeeper's inn. It was the innkeeper—the unsung, heroic caretaker—who did the hard, day-in-and-day-out job of taking care of the injured traveler.

The girls and I decided to use an agency to provide someone to come and stay with Mike. It really was an easy job. Someone just needed to be here to make sure Mike did not leave the house or yard and to make sure that he did not harm himself. There was no housework to do and no cooking—I prepared all Mike's meals and left them in the refrigerator—and at this time, Mike still sort of used the bathroom, so generally there were no Depend diapers to change.

The agency we called came out, assessed the situation, and said they would be glad to help. After all, their job was to supply in-home caretakers. The agency was very nice and appeared to be accommodating of our needs. We requested male caretakers thinking they would be better able to handle Mike's sometimes aggressive behaviors.

The first caretaker they sent us worked out well for several months. We were all happy. The girls still stayed with Mike some but had more free time to take care of their homes and children. I was happy at work knowing that a "professional" was caring for Mike.

One day, the caretaker said, "May I ask you a personal question?"

No Sugar Added!

"Sure," I said.

"Was Mike always this hateful?" he asked.

My heart broke as I assured him that Mike had never, ever been hateful and in fact was the kindest, most gentle, and most thoughtful person I had ever known.

Then came the day when the caretaker called in sick and did not show up. The caretaker continued to call in sick and then finally admitted that he did not want to be with Mike. He said, "Mike is just too mean to be around."

Another caretaker was provided by the agency. He fit in well. He brought in pictures from the past to try to engage Mike in conversations. Mike did not converse with him—but then again, at that point, Mike was not conversing with anyone, although he could still say words. The words just had no logic or connection to reality. They were just random words. But the caretaker tried. We were so very grateful. Then that caretaker started not showing up on time. Apparently, he was very busy. We overlooked his tardiness because we were so happy that he was willing to be there at all. He started calling in sick. We were still limping along, hoping things would work out.

Then came the day when I received a telephone call at work from my daughter. The caretaker had just called her and said, "Mike chased me around the house with a knife. I am out of here. Never coming back," and hung up. We never saw or heard from him again. Fortunately, Kawai was able to drop everything and race right over the house to be with Mike.

We were a little puzzled about the knife comment because several years before, we had "weapon-proofed" the house. We had removed all knives, all walking sticks, and the Haitian machetes— we had quite a few of these because they were gifts given to us by my father from his travels—from the house and stored them in Shani's garage. (One day, Jeff was working in the garage and asked

Lucid

Shani, puzzled, "Why is there a collection of kitchen knives and walking sticks in our garage?" Shani replied that she was storing them for her mom.) It turned out that the knife that Mike had used to chase the caretaker out of the house was a butter knife. Any excuse will do when you don't want to do a job anymore! The bottom line was that the grand "hire a caretaker experiment" had failed. We were back to square one. We needed to continue to *"be strong and courageous. Do not fear or be in dread of them,* where I just replaced "them" with "demented times", *for it is the Lord your God who goes with you. He will not leave you or forsake you."*

But you see, Lord—this journey, this traveling down the dementia trail, is not a journey that Mike and I chose to go on!

****

Side note: A few days after the end of the "hire a caretaker experiment," Shani and Brooke were over at the house, watching Mike.

"What happened to the babysitters that used to come over and be with Grandpa?" Brooke asked Shani.

Shani answered that they no longer wanted to be with grandpa.

"Why do we still stay with him?" Brooke asked.

Shani's answer, "Because we are family," said it all.

Chapter 4

2012-2014: Home Alone

Caregiver Prayer

*Though the fig tree does not bud and there are no grapes on
the vines,
Though the olive crop fails and the fields produce no food,
Though there are no sheep in the pen
And no cattle in the stalls,
Yet I will rejoice in the Lord
I will be joyful in God my Savior.
The Sovereign Lord is my strength;
He makes my feet like the feet of a deer,
He enables me to tread on the heights.
—Habakkuk 3:17-19*

Lucid

The grand "hire a caretaker experiment" had failed. Mike could not do any daily functions such as getting dressed, eating, going to the bathroom, or keeping himself clean. But most importantly, he could not keep himself safe. All this had to be done for him.

We all agreed it had been a very nice idea to hire someone to stay with Mike, and we were devastated that it had not worked out. But reality was reality. If no one would stay, then no one would stay.

(A quick side note: In a way, it was easier not to have someone come in and stay with Mike because when someone was coming in, I always felt compelled to make sure the house was cleaned up and ready for a "visitor" before I left for work. In contrast, I never felt any compulsion to make sure the kitchen floor was mopped if it was one of the girls who was coming over to stay with Mike!)

The writing was on the wall! There was only one option left that seemed feasible. It was time for me to retire and stay home with Mike 24/7.

Whether or not to retire was a tough decision. Looking on the bright side, I was very aware of, and thankful for, the fact that, because of Kawai and Shani's physical proximity and infinite willingness to help, I had been very fortunate to work as long as I had after Mike's dementia diagnosis.

****

The girls agreed to go back to watching Mike full time for a few months until I worked out a logical retirement plan

Honestly, I had never, ever given a single thought to retirement. At times over the years, Mike would say something about our planning for retirement, but I could not conceive of not working, so the conversation was never pursued. At work, I had noticed that more and more of my coworkers were my children's contemporaries and not contemporaries of mine. I vaguely realized that maybe sometime in the far future I would have to stop working—like maybe when my coworkers were the age of my grandchildren.

Every day, without fail, as I drove into the entrance of the Johnson Space Center, I said a quick, "Thank you, God, for my job." The awe of actually having the job never left me. I figured that the reason why I felt so blessed was that it had been so hard to find a job in the first place that actually having such a great job had never stopped feeling like a miracle.

*****

Many years before, as I was getting ready to leave home and head off to college, my father asked me, "Shannon, have you given any thought to what you are going to major in?"

"Of course!" I replied. "I am going to major in chemistry! I am going to be a chemist!"

"If you major in chemistry, you will need to take education courses as well, so that you can at least get a teaching job." (This was a very realistic bit of advice from a father to a daughter in 1959.)

"Oh no, Father. I do not need to do that," I told him. "I am not going to be a teacher. I am going to work as a chemist in a laboratory. There is a desperate need for scientists—especially chemists—right now. When I get out of college, don't you worry! I will get a job making over ten thousand dollars a year!" (This was the largest salary I could visualize in 1959.)

In college, I majored in chemistry. It was the early sixties and, yes, many times in my upper-level chemistry courses I was the only female in the class, but I never really thought about that.

I had never known anyone who had worked as a chemist, so two weeks before I graduated in August of 1963, I went up to my inorganic chemistry professor and asked, "I am about to graduate, and I would like to know how a person gets a job as a chemist."

"You want to work?" he asked me with bemusement.

Taken aback, I replied, "Yes, of course. That's why I majored in chemistry."

"But you are a woman. No one is going to hire you!"

Unfortunately, my professor was right. My father was right. My first job after college graduation was changing diapers while working third shift in a nursing home.

During this time, while on my short break at one o'clock in the morning, I would stand outside under the blazing stars and implore God to provide me with "real" work—work in a lab with test tubes and beakers, where I would be able to delve into the mysteries of the universe.

Finally, my prayers were answered, and I landed a job in a real laboratory, but the two hundred and fifty dollars a month certainly did not add up to ten thousand dollars a year. That would have to wait until after fifteen years of continuous employment, after I had completed graduate school, and after anti-discrimination legislation passed by the US Congress. Only in January 1978, when I started to work for NASA at the Johnson Space Center, did I make more than the ten thousand dollars a year that I had so optimistically told my father I was going to earn.

Thirty-four years later, on January 31, 2012, I went through the checkout process at the Johnson Space Center, turned in my badge, and then—in the gray misty fog of a Houston winter morning—drove several times up and down all the roads at the Johnson Space Center. All things come to an end. Even working for NASA.

Finally, I drove out the back gate, no longer belonging. I was now an outsider.

I was home in a few minutes. That morning, both girls had stayed with Mike. By the time I arrived home, they had packed up,

No Sugar Added!

buckled their kids into their car seats, and were ready to head out. As soon as I pulled into the driveway, they waved goodbye.

It was now just Mike and me, 24/7. I walked into the house. Mike had attempted to defecate into the kitchen trash can. He had missed. Feces had rolled onto the floor. From that moment on, Mike wore Depend diapers twenty-four hours a day. Welcome to my new full-time, all-day, everyday job.

Suddenly, the realization hit me—I had come full circle back to where I had started in my career. But the upside was that now, at least, the diapers that I was changing were disposable pull-ups and not the washable cotton ones the size and texture of dish towels that were held together with large safety pins. Back in 1963 when I had started my first job, changing those cloth diapers had been quite challenging. Sometimes it had meant chasing a naked person down dark hallways with large safety pins in one hand and a cloth diaper in the other. Modern technology, in the form of Depend diapers, was indeed wonderful.

When I mentioned the full circle of my working career to my daughters, they immediately exclaimed together, "We are so glad that we did not start our working careers changing diapers!" That was so true. Both girls had had career type jobs after college graduation, Kawi as a social worker and Shani as a computer programmer.

Several times that first evening of being "home alone," I thought about the biblical verse *"I have learned to be content whatever the circumstances. I know what it is to be in need, and I know what it is to have plenty. I have learned the secret of being content in any and every situation, whether well fed or hungry, whether living in plenty or in want. I can do all this through Him who gives in strength!"* (Phil 4:11b–13)

My own ability to recall things was still sparkly clear. I was able to remember all the past times when things looked dark, and there seemed to be no light shining into the future, such as when I was refused employment because of being female or when I was fired for getting pregnant—the list could go on forever. I remembered how the Lord had provided strength to just live day by day, and I was at peace knowing that every day of my new caretaker job, I would be given the strength to persevere.

That night, I read the evening prayer of day three from *A Diary of Private Prayer* by John Baille. I read the line: "In thy presence, O God, I think not only of myself, but of others, my fellow men: Of those who are manning difficult stations or lonely outposts of thy kingdom." The phrase "lonely outposts of thy kingdom," resonated deeply within me. It was the perfect job description for my new, full-time caregiving job.

****

Intellectually, I had understood that I still had a lot to learn about caregiving, but I had never imagined how steep the learning curve would be!

The first few weeks of total incontinence were horrific. In the morning, the floor of the bedroom where Mike had been all night would be covered with feces. The adult diapers did not totally contain the diarrhea. The first thing I did every morning was to take scraper and scrape feces off the floor. It took only one fall, after which I ended up with a bruised thigh and arm, for me to learn that urine on a laminate floor is very slick and difficult to see. After cleaning the floor, I would clean Mike up, which meant a quick shower, if Mike was in a "shower amenable" mood. If not, then lots of baby wipes, clean clothes, and new diapers. Every day, I breathed a prayer of thankfulness for having had the carpet ripped out a few years earlier and replaced with a laminate floor. Even my superb imagination failed me when I tried to think of what it would have been like had the floor still been carpeted.

Mike was not docile when it came to being cleaned and changed. It required of me a lot of quick in and out movements and fancy footwork to avoid his attempts to fend off the cleaner—that would be me. Finally, the morning came when I called the Alzheimer's Association in utter frustration and asked, "How do caretakers manage incontinence? Are there any standard procedures? Are there any tricks of the trade that I could use?" I launched into a vividly detailed description of what my morning that far had entailed.

First, I had awakened to the strong smell of a sewer. No, it was not a broken sewage line; it was an extremely unpleasant bathroom and bedroom. There were feces on the floor.

There were feces in the sink, on the counter, and on the dresser. (Oddly enough, the toilet contained no feces.)

There were feces on the doorframes.

There were dried feces on the blankets.

OK, I will admit to an ever-so-slight exaggeration—but not by much!

I had gotten Mike into the shower and—after thirty minutes of work using gloves, rags, Lysol, and Clorox—the bedroom was once again fresh as a daisy, and Mike was clean and in new diaper and fresh clothes.

After listening to my description of the morning, the pleasant lady on the phone told me, "I have no idea how to help, but I will see what I can find out." Later in the day, she sent me a link to a generic web page that said that many times the demented patient was incontinent, but it did not say a thing about how to manage it as a caretaker. I called numerous care facilities and asked for helpful hints on how they handled situations like this. "I will call you back," was always the answer. No one ever called back.

Lucid

Luckily, I had a daughter—a very smart daughter. Shani said, "Why don't you give Dad a probiotic every day and see if that helps?" I put a probiotic into Mike's daily ice cream cone, and it was a miracle! That word is not used lightly. From then on, Mike's feces were semisolid and stayed in the diapers. Hallelujah! A caretaker cannot ask for much more than that! As I said, it was a miracle. And then I pushed the envelope a little further. Sometimes when I desperately needed a short respite, I would put an Imodium into the ice cream cone and take an "Imodium vacation" for the day.

One morning, I was scraping "cow patties" off the bedroom floor. I thought about what I had just finished reading in Ezekiel, where God commanded Ezekiel to use human dung for cooking. It seemed to me that remembering this divine commandment at that moment had to be more than mere coincidence. But no matter how hard I tried; I was not able to tease out any spiritual relevance! I am still pondering that moment.

****

Incontinence was only one of a constant stream of new challenges that demanded solutions.

For ten years, Mike had been able to manage eating utensils—even though that gradually meant using just a spoon. And then the time came when he couldn't manage even a spoon. But fingers—he had fingers, and they worked great! If we could get the food into his hand and wrap his fingers around it, he would get the food to his mouth and eat it. We got very creative with finger foods. Bananas were super. But if we didn't supervise the process, the bananas would have just as good a chance of being sat on as being chewed. Certain sandwiches, such as grilled cheese, breakfast bars, and pizza—there was an endless supply of finger food that Mike could manage to eat. He could also drink if a straw was placed in his mouth. A drinking container with a lid and a straw worked great if we could get his hands wrapped around the container. He would clutch the container and suck on the straw. Of course, sometimes he would hurl the drinking container across the room instead, just like he sometimes hurled his plate of finger foods. The only thing that he consistently ate without making a mess was an ice cream cone.

Mike could walk, but sometimes he ended up on the floor. I did not classify it as falling—it was more like he forgot how to locomote and wilted. In all the times I found him on the floor, he was never hurt. But there was the problem of getting him up again. If he ended up on the floor, he could not get up by himself. When I first started finding Mike on the floor, he was still a large man—much too large for me to pull up onto his feet by myself. The first time I found him on the floor, both of our sons-in-law were out of town. I got Mike into a comfortable sitting position on the floor and just waited until they returned to Houston that evening. Working together, Jeff and Kirk were able to get Mike up and walking again.

The next time I found Mike on the floor, a perfect solution popped into my head. I found the inflatable mattress we used for camping and rolled it out on the floor next to Mike. I then rolled him onto it. I plugged in the air pump, and it inflated quickly. I put a pillow under Mike's head, and there was Mike lying in comfort until a strong son-in-law could drop by and help me get Mike upright again.

Only once did this method not work, and I had to come up with something different. Caleb was spending the night. He and I were fast asleep on the big, blow-up mattress just outside Mike's closed door. Mike's screaming startled me awake. I ran in to investigate. Mike was on all fours in the middle of the bedroom, like a dog. He was trying to move but couldn't. It was like he no longer knew how to get his limbs to move. What to do?

I took a plastic trunk from the closet and slid it under Mike's chest. I then was able to slide the trunk, with Mike on it, over to the bed—again so grateful for the laminate floors! I took a pair of his lounging pants, wrapped them around his waist, and rolled and heaved him onto the bed. As soon as he was lying down, he was out cold. I covered him, shoved a pillow under the mattress to keep him from rolling out of bed, and went back to sleep.

In the morning, Mike was up and walking around. The entire episode had been so bizarre. I was surprised by how disturbed I was to see Mike in the "dog position" and not able to move.

Personal cleanliness and grooming were a huge challenge. My daughters and I had slightly different techniques for changing Mike's diapers. The big difference in our techniques was that they would wait until Mike was compliant. In contrast, I had things to do, so when Mike needed to be changed, I was primed to get the task accomplished. (As Shani pointed out to me many times, I was not the right personality type to be a caretaker. I was too goal oriented. As my daughters repeated constantly to me, "You need to just go with the flow" with no pun intended by their statement.

When Mike needed to be changed, I got out a new diaper, baby wipes, gloves, clean lounging pants, and a new shirt for Mike. (Depend diapers were good at liquid retention, but sometimes there was more liquid than they could handle, and urine would wick up the shirt. That is why we always had to be ready to change his shirt.) Then I would get behind Mike as he was marching around the room and maybe singing nonsense syllables at the top of his lungs and, with one fell swoop, pull down his lounging pants and the diaper. Then I would back him up to the seat of his recliner, which I had already covered with a disposable pad, and would gently push him down into a sitting position. Next, I would synchronize my dart in,

No Sugar Added!

dart out movements to Mike's agitated kicks so his legs and feet would miss hitting me while I yanked off the pants and diaper. If the diaper contained feces, then I took the diaper to the toilet and rolled out the fecal matter. Of course, after this, the floor would have to be mopped with bleach. All the trash was bagged in plastic grocery bags before going into a garbage bag. Next, Mike's feet would be placed into the clean diapers and then lifted and pushed through the legs of the clean lounge pants. The next step was to get Mike upright by placing my feet in front of his so that he would not slip and then pulling him upright. As soon as he was upright, I would clean him with baby wipes and then pull up the diaper and lounge pants. Mission accomplished. Once again, Mike was dry and clean. Of course, the mission would need to be repeated in just a few hours. An optimist would have thought of it as job security!

The time came when, because of Mike's stiff resistance, just one person could not get Mike into a standing position, and then it became a two-person job, with a person on each side of Mike, hands under his armpits and hoisting him to a standing position. If Mike got his knees locked, he could walk. If not, we scooted him to the nearby bed, lowered him onto it, and changed him while he was lying down.

Have I mentioned how fortunate it was that Kawai and Shani and their husbands lived so close by?

To express my appreciation for their help and to try to simplify their lives when they were in charge of Mike, I put together a Cold-Water Box. I took a plastic washbasin and on one side taped a big, neatly printed sign on fluorescent yellow paper that said Cold Water Box. In the box were a couple of fresh diapers, a box of disposable gloves, disposable shoe covers, a packet of wet wipes, grocery bags (used to dispose of the soiled diapers and wipes) and a spray can of room deodorizer—everything needed to keep Mike nice and clean in one handy place. On the other side of the washbasin, on florescent bright-green paper, I printed the verse, *"And if anyone gives even a cup of cold water to one of the least of these little ones, [remember—there are none more least than the demented!] who is my disciple, truly I tell you, that person will certainly not lose their reward."* (Matthew 10:42)

Seeing the labeled box for the first time, the girls responded in their typical fashion by rolling their eyes. I pointed out to them that, when you were doing an unpleasant task, it was very important to remember why you were doing it! Again, I got an eye roll in response.

I got Mike's face washed and his teeth brushed every day. Even these simple tasks were not without drama. I got very adept at not letting Mike grab the wet washcloth and fling it in my face. Sometimes he would bite down hard on the toothbrush, and it was a major effort to get it removed from his mouth. The toothpaste, he just swallowed.

Showers were a very big deal. When I managed to shower him, it was worthy of a self-congratulatory email sent to the kids. "Guess what I accomplished today?" I'd ask. A positive reply of, "Job well done, Mom!" made my day.

It got so that I could sense when Mike would let me shower him. There was no point in trying at any other time. First, I had to maneuver him into the bathroom. This was tough. For some reason, he always resisted going through the bathroom door. He would grab the doorframe and push back as I tried to maneuver him in. I would have to restrain his hands and keep him upright with my body pressed behind his back to get him through the door. Then I would undress him, turn on the shower, check the water temperature, and then wrap his hands around the vertical shower bar so that he would not fall. After all this, I lifted his leg up and over the tub and placed it on the rubber bathmat in the tub. Then,

No Sugar Added!

by pushing slightly on his side and tapping the rear of his other leg (I felt like a horse trainer), he would lift it into the tub.

He always seemed to derive so much satisfaction from the warm water cascading over him. He would make washing motions with his hands, and he would moan with what sounded like pleasure. I would soap him down and then rinse him off. I let him stand in the shower as long as the hot water lasted. He was always compliant about getting out. I would dry him off and then get behind him for support to keep him upright and walk him to his chair where, with a gentle nudge, I got him seated. Then I would dress him. Usually, right after a shower was the easiest time to get him shaved. And right after a shower was the only time I could get his fingernails and toenails cut.

The time came when I no longer felt comfortable with Mike standing in the shower, so it was time for a new plan. I took a shower chair and set it sideways in the tub. I knew that there was no way I could get Mike into the tub and seated on the shower chair if it were facing to the front of the shower. Then I got Mike next to the tub, turned him around so that the back of his legs was touching the side of the tub, and gently pushed him into a sitting position on the chair. Yes, the lower parts of his legs were outside the tub, but the rest of him was inside. Then I showered the part of his body that was inside the tub. I put his feet, which were outside the tub, into a plastic washbasin and washed them. (As I was washing his feet, I thought of the middle of the verse 1 Timothy 5:9–10, which says, *"No widow. . . well known for good deeds, bringing up children, showing hospitality, washing the feet of the Lord's people."*! I wasn't a widow, but Mike was one of the Lord's people. I was doing a lot of foot washing—but, to tell the truth, I never felt very godly doing it! (During this period of time, while I was thinking about all foot washing I was doing, there was a clip on the news about the Pope washing the feet of the homeless.

Lucid

It occurred to me that maybe I should let the Pope know that if he wanted to a real foot washing challenge, he should try washing the feet of the belligerent demented!) After drying Mike's feet, I would pull him upright and dry him all over. Then I maneuvered him back to his chair, where I dressed him.

One morning, as I tried to get Mike into the shower and he was soaking me with urine and spit, this caretaker's chant popped full blown into my head:

Caretaker's Chant

Sticks and stones may break my bones
But
Urine and spittle will not hurt me!

I found this chant, repeated like a mantra, very comforting while I was trying to get Mike into the shower. (I will modestly admit being the author of this chant. It is not copyrighted, so please feel free to use it if you are in a situation where you would find it helpful.)

****

Mike's ability to speak diminished to almost zero. Once in a great while he would utter an isolated word. What was strange was that more often than not, this word was a foul word that, in the over forty years Mike and I had lived together, I had never heard him say. It was disturbing to hear him utter words like that. Then the words stopped, and the whistling started. You would ask him a question and try to engage him in conversation, but he would just whistle. It was very interesting, but also very strange. We assumed it was his attempt at "conversation." If the girls or the grandkids tried to talk to him, the answer was a whistled "melody," but it was not a melody that was recognizable to anyone else. And every time I heard Mike whistle, I would think of God calling us: "*He whistles for those at the end of the earth.*" (Isaiah 5:26)

I decided to remove Mike from Medicare part B. After all, we were never going to get him to a doctor's office again and, if he needed medical care, he was covered by our Blue Cross policy. I called Medicare. The person I talked to insisted that he had to talk to Mike. I explained that Mike did not speak. He still insisted that Mike be put on the phone. Once again, I explained that Mike did not talk—he only whistled. Once again, he insisted that Mike be put on the phone. I held the phone to Mike's ear and told him to speak. He whistled. After his mini-concert, I got back on the phone. The Medicare person said, "That was very interesting. I have been told of that happening with people with dementia, but I have never heard it before."

After I sent in my power of attorney and a written request to remove Mike from part B, he was removed.

Every night, I always said to Mike, "Have a good night, Mike, and remember how much God loves you—and I love you, also."

One night, for the first and only time, there was a response. Mike motioned for me to come close. He said, "Listen," and then started to whistle. He took his hand and started to gently rub my arm. I replied, "Thank you, Mike. I know you love me, also." He closed his eyes in peace.

But in the morning, Mike grabbed his urine-logged diaper and hit me across the face with it, spattering urine everywhere.

****

It was true that at times, it seemed our life was overcast and cloudy, but most of the time it was the silver lining of these clouds

Lucid

that filled our vision! (I know that sliver-lined clouds are a cliché, but clichés exist because often they describe a truth!)

The first summer I stayed home alone with Mike, we were given not just an ordinary silver lining, but a diamond-encrusted, golden lining. Two new grandchildren—the twins, Davey and Danny—joined our family.

After Kawai had graduated with a master's degree in social work, her first job was working with foster children. At that time, she decided that when she was in a situation in her life where it was possible, she wanted to become a foster parent. Just before I retired, she and Kirk decided that being foster parents was "now or never." They put in an application, went through the training, and were certified. Kawai's vision had been to foster children roughly the same age as her other three children. She and Kirk definitely had no plans to foster babies.

The first call they received for a placement was for three-week-old twin boys that needed a place to stay for the night. Kawai said yes. Kirk rushed to Walmart to buy cribs, and our lives were forever changed. After a year, Davey and Danny became available for adoption. Kawai and Kirk adopted them—and just like that, Mike and I now had eight grandchildren!

Just after the twins arrived, we formulated plans for the annual cabin trip. The "before the twins" plan had been for Shani and Kawai to alternate, each spending a week at the cabin and a week at home with Mike. Since Kawai was taking care of two very young babies anyway, she offered to stay home with Mike so that Shani and I could take the other kids to the cabin spending only a week. So that is what we did.

Shani, I, and six of the grandchildren had a great trip. Kawai, spending the day with her demented father and two babies, survived. Jeff and Kirk took turns staying with Mike at night so that Kawai and the twins could go home and have a sort of break—

No Sugar Added!

although, as we were all rapidly finding out, one never really gets a "break" when it comes to caring for twin babies.

Many times, on the trip, Shani and I commented, "Can you believe it was just one year ago that we drove Dad to the cabin?"

And then at various points along the way, we noted

That's where we could not get Dad into the car.

That's the motel where he defecated all over the floor.

That's where we could not get Dad out of the restroom.

So many points of interest on the Dementia Trail!

That cabin week was very long for Kawai, and very short for Shani, the grandchildren, and me.

On the return trip, we stopped by Carlsbad Caverns. Then, as we drove east down I-10 and headed home, our iPhones picked up the feed from the video cameras that had been installed at the house. It was a little awe-inspiring watching Kawai manage two small babies and one roaming father with dementia! And never once was she observed pulling her hair out.

I texted Kawai: "The kids loved Carlsbad Caverns. Shani wanted to make the turn to Big Bend this afternoon, but I talked her out of it. I heard Dad calling!"

Kawai replied: "Just so you know what to expect:

Your house is a disaster and smells like urine—maybe it is partly the fault of the baby diapers, but the adult ones smell worse. True, they all go in the outside trash, but the smell remains.

Dad is a mess—literally. He was OK until this morning. Gross, gross, but he did not want to take a shower. Luckily, you are due home in a few hours and my conscience is not too bothered by letting him be yucky for one day.

Dad somehow smashed up the entire contents of a Rice Krispies box this morning and spread it all over the house. He mashed it up very well. (I know—my fault for leaving it in his path.)

Lucid

There are pizza crusts thrown about from Dad's lunch that I have not gotten around to picking up yet.

The dishes were done once, but I haven't gotten around to doing them again.

One of my shoes is missing, but judging from what was in Dad's hat, I may not want it back even if I find it."

I texted a reply: "Thanks for letting me know what to expect. I would be lying if I said I was thrilled to be coming home, but duty calls, so I will be there."

****

If I had been asked, right after starting my full-time job of 24/7 caretaking, for one word that fit my new life, I would have immediately replied, "Isolation."

To me, at that time, the word *isolation* seemed to be the perfect word to sum up my existence.

Isolation, defined by *Merriam-Webster*, is "the state of being in a place or situation that is separate from others."

Isolation connotes a state of discontent.

Isolation depletes body, mind, and spirit.

I was committed to being there with Mike twenty-four hours a day, seven days a week. After dropping by the first time, only one visitor ever dropped by a second time. It was just too unpleasant to be in the presence of a walking body from which personhood had been hollowed out. It was not pleasant to be around Mike, who might be sprawled across a chair snoring or maybe sitting in a chair and folding the same towel over and over while repeatedly moaning a nonsensical chant or—even more disturbingly—suddenly appearing naked.

No Sugar Added!

Fortunately for my sanity, the girls and the grandkids spent a lot of time with us at the house, but there were times when even they were uncomfortable in the presence of Mike.

For instance, one Sunday evening, while Kawai, Caleb, and Shani were at the house, Mike had one of his screaming fits, where he shouted obscenities and yelled over and over, "Help me! Help me! Oh God!"

Caleb covered his ears, ran, and cowered in a corner of the kitchen, sobbing and saying, "I want to go home, go home!" And I cried because Caleb, at this point, was the grandchild who was the most accepting of Mike—maybe because he had never known Mike any other way. Caleb consistently hugged Mike whenever he came over to the house. And now that fragile bond appeared to have been severed.

The next day when Caleb came over, as soon as he saw Mike, he covered his ears, ran, and hid.

Fortunately, Caleb did not stay frightened of Mike for long. A few days later, Caleb came over just after I had mopped the bathroom floor with bleach. Caleb ran in to use the bathroom and slipped and fell on the wet floor. Mike started moving toward Caleb's cries. Caleb held up his hand and said, "Stop, Grandpa! Don't get hurt." Then Caleb got up, took Mike by the hand, and led him to where he thought his grandpa wanted to go.

Because of my life of isolation, I found myself forgetting how to carry on a conversation with other people. When I went out to lunch with acquaintances from my previous life of paid employment, I would always be asked the question, "Well, what exciting things are you doing now that you are retired?"

Of course, I answered the question truthfully. "Taking care of my husband with dementia 24/7."

Inevitably, that was a conversation stopper.

Lucid

I told Kawai about how this answer stopped all conversation, and she (the English major—have I mentioned how handy it is to have a daughter who majored in English and loves to write?) wrote out a speech for me to use as an answer that I memorized:

"Well, I pretty much take care of my husband, who was diagnosed with dementia eight years ago. But my daughters help me out, and I've been fortunate to be able to take my grandchildren on some wonderful trips. So far, I have been able on two separate trips to take four of the grandchildren, two by two, to China. (Why China? I had been born there and started kindergarten in China. My mother had grown up in China because my grandfather was a missionary doctor there. I wanted the grandkids to connect with their ancestors so traveled with them to China.) One of my daughters is so very glad that I am home so that I can help her with the twin baby boys she just adopted. My days are filled with meaningful tasks."

I used this speech and was grateful that it did help to keep conversations flowing.

One day, as I was organizing our books, I came across one of the books written by my grandfather when he was a doctor working at a leprosy clinic in China, which was titled *Unclean, Unclean.*

Lepers, before the advent of sulfa drugs, were ostracized by society and had to have been the premier, historical example of social isolation.

It occurred to me that socially, dementia is the modern-day equivalent of leprosy. Demented people and the caretakers of the demented are basically shunned by normal society.

A story printed in the July 11, 2014 issue of *The Week* reinforced my observation. The story told how a group of Tea Party Republicans snuck into a nursing home in order to photograph the demented spouse of a candidate in a hotly contested race for a Senate seat. The images were put online in an attempt to smear the candidate. Obviously, the ultraconservative Tea Partiers had forgotten Proverbs 17:5a: *"Whoever mocks the poor [insert "demented] shows contempt for their maker."* I rest my case!

Today, the person with dementia does not have to cry out, "Unclean! Unclean!" to maintain their isolation. Instead, the presence of the demented cries out, "Crazy! Crazy!" and that is enough for all society to give them a wide berth. And, incidentally, the caretaker, who is contaminated by "crazy-life fallout," is also given a wide berth.

And for both, the historical lepers and today's people with dementia, there was/is no cure—only isolation.

It occurred to me that if my grandfather were alive today, he could write a book about dementia and title it *Crazy, Crazy.*

****

After a few months of being home alone, I realized that if asked for one word to describe my daily existence, I would no longer answer with the word *isolation*. My answer would be *solitude*.

The words *solitude* and *isolation* are not synonyms. They are totally different. Solitude is a state of being alone without being lonely. It is a state that leads to inner awareness. Solitude is a state actively sought out by many people to be used as a time for reflection. Solitude is a refreshing time to renew ourselves. Solitude restores both the body and mind.

I discovered that solitude was another silver lining to my life—true, not as diamond-encrusted as the golden lining of the twins but nevertheless, solid silver!

At times, the image that I most identified with in my role of Mike's caretaker was that of being a monk, living in a monastery during the Dark Ages. Secluded, solitary, and listening for the still, small voice of the Lord. But what was missing from my existence, compared to that of the monks, was the structure of monastic life—the rhythm of set times for set activities such as prayer at five thirty am, work at ten, worship at eight pm. There was absolutely no rhythm to my life while caring for Mike—only chaotic flexibility. Not even sleep in the middle of the night could be counted on because Mike had lost all vestiges of circadian rhythm. We worked hard to keep structure to Mike's day, but nothing we did helped. For instance, meals were provided at normal times, but this was not enough to cue his body to function on a normal, twenty-four-hour cycle.

Because Mike's day had no rhythm, I, the caretaker, could not count on the circadian rhythm giving order to my own life. The controlling function of my life was the lack of circadian rhythm in Mike's. There was no rhyme or reason as to when Mike would start screaming, immediately yanking me from the depths of sound slumber and making me rush to him to discover the reason for the screaming. There was no set time when Mike might need to be changed. In order to try to prevent bedsores, I had to maintain constant vigilance to make sure that Mike did not wear a soiled diaper for long.

I had asked for medication to help Mike sleep through the night but was refused. I was told, "Sleeping medications have to be avoided in demented persons. Such medications only exasperate the demented condition."

"Really?" I thought. "You think it could get any worse?"

I stumbled upon the realization that I shared a very important aspect of the lives of monks—and that was fasting!

Monks fast as a spiritual discipline. They go without food for specified periods of time in order to draw themselves closer to God. While reading Isaiah, I realized that I was doing one better than monks! I was fasting every day, and not just for specified periods. No, I was not going without food—I was daily practicing

No Sugar Added!

Caretaker Fasting, a term that popped into my head as I read the passage.

I hear you asking, "What in the world is Caretaking Fasting?" Isaiah recorded the description:

Caretaker Fasting

Is not this the kind of fasting I have chosen?
. . . . .
Is it not to share your food with the hungry,
And to provide the wanderer with shelter—
When you see the naked, to clothe them
And to not turn away from your own flesh and blood?
—Isaiah 58:6a, 7

What a perfect description of my everyday life! I gave Mike three meals a day, plus numerous ice cream cones. Daily, I provided Mike with safe shelter as he wandered hither and yon over house and yard. I put clothes on him whenever he ambled by naked. I did all this because he was "bone of my bone, flesh of my flesh!"

There was an extra silver lining to solitude's silver lining; it was the gift of time for reflection. There was plenty of time to ponder the meaning of Mike's and my current situation. Without the pressing responsibilities of "real life"—family, work, etc.—I had more time than I had ever had before in my life to reflect on what I read daily in the Bible, just like a monk in a monastery!

****

My daily habit of reading the Bible stared in early childhood because of an intense desire to learn how to swim.

Lucid

The summer after I was in the fourth grade, a new pool had opened nearby in a local park. They were offering swimming lessons. After much begging on my part, my father enrolled me. I went for my first lesson. There were two pools. A big pool filled with lots of teachers and cavorting kids and a much smaller pool with no kids, no teachers, and that was empty and had just two diving boards—one high and one low. My teacher trooped his line of kids out to the smaller pool. He lined us up by the ladder that went up to the high diving board and then he dove into the water. The first kid climbed the ladder and dove in. Then the second. Then the third. It was my turn. I climbed up and jumped in. I sank. I bobbed up. I sank. I bobbed up.

The teacher yelled, "Wells, do you know how to swim?" I shook my head no as I sank once again. On my next bob up, the teacher extended a pole, and I grabbed it. He pulled me out. His first words were, "Wells, don't you know that this is the advanced diving class?" I shook my head no and he sent me back to get dressed. That was the end of my swimming dreams at that pool, because there was no room in any of the other classes.

Later that summer, I was in a swimming pool at the YMCA. My friend across the street invited me to go swimming at the Y with her church youth group. After making sure that females could wear bathing suits and not swim naked (I had heard that all male swimmers had to swim naked at the Y), I said yes. I was so excited.

In the pool, the girls divided themselves into two groups: one swimming and one just splashing. I wanted to be in the swimming group. I imitated the girls who were swimming across the pool. One asked if I could swim. I said yes, and she told me to swim with her across the pool.

I said, "In a minute." To myself, I said that I needed to do a just a wee bit of practicing. I started across the pool. Some girls were watching. I just had to swim across the pool. The other side was so far away. I prayed, "God, let me swim across the pool. Let me swim across the pool, and I will read four chapters in the Bible every day." As I swam across the pool, the words "four chapters every day" repeated themselves over and over in my brain, acting as a coordinating mantra to my kicking legs and wind milling arms. I made it across the pool. Now I had a vow to keep: four chapters every day.

That night, I started with Genesis 1:1 and read the first four chapters of Genesis. The next night, I read the next four chapters, skipping nothing—not even the long lists of genealogy. Summer turned to fall, to winter, to spring, and back to summer—and every day, I read four chapters. After all, when you make a vow to God, you kept it! And then finally I read Revelation 21:6a: *"It is done. I am the Alpha and Omega, the beginning and the end."* After a few more verses, there it was—the end of the Bible. I had done it. I had read every word in the Bible! I closed the cover of my King James Version of the Bible and thought—that's that. I did it! I read the entire Bible. Now I know everything about God and what God has to say! Now what? Oh, the arrogance of being eleven! Never again would I face life with such absolute "know-it-all" confidence! The rest of my life has been one long journey of realizing more and more how little I know about and understand God.

Then there was a niggling doubt. My vow had been to read four chapters of the Bible every day. It had not been to read the Bible all the way through. I realized that when I made my vow, I had forgotten to put an ending on it! Was I still committed to reading four chapters every day? (At least I had not vowed to sacrifice the first thing that came to meet me when I arrived home!) Just to be safe—after all, making vows to God was very serious—I started back at the beginning, back at Genesis 1:1. Then I had an amazing epiphany: I did not know everything God had to say. In fact, as I started back through the Bible, I had the constant, recurring thought, "Have I really read this before?" And a funny thing happened. Over time, "the tyranny of the vow" lost its force. I continued reading after I had read the Bible for the first time because I longed to know more and more about God, and I found that in the hard stretches of life—and most of life is a hard stretch—this is what kept me going.

But my "vow" had taught me several valuable lessons:

I needed to be very careful of what I vowed. (Incidentally, I only ever made one other vow in my life—and that was to be with Mike, for better or for worse!)

The Bible was full of stories that were never mentioned in polite 1950s society, much less preached about!

Daily reading of the Bible should remain a major part of my life. And so it has been. Because of family and work, I did not read the entire Bible every year, and there were short stretches where I did not even read the Bible daily, but there were many years where I did read through the Bible.

This vow, which was made so many years ago and which turned into a habit, was what made it possible to navigate and survive the journey of taking care of a husband with dementia.

****

I couldn't stop comparing and contrasting my life to that of a monk. Monks living in their monasteries had a purpose—to daily seek after God. My days locked up in my "monastery," seemed devoid of purpose—days spent working hard, doing three or four loads of laundry, feeding Mike, changing Mike, and mopping the floors—seemed totally devoid of any purpose and of meaning. I shed my feeling of futility one day when the verse *"Therefore, my dear brothers and sisters, stand firm. Let nothing move you. Always give yourselves fully to the work of the Lord, because you know*

No Sugar Added!

that your labor in the Lord is not in vain." (I Cor 15:58) got stuck in my head, constantly repeating on an endless loop over and over again.

Why? Because all my labor was "the work of the Lord." The logic of this statement was as straightforward as a geometric theorem. (At long last, all the time spent proving theorems in geometry so many years ago came in handy in a real-life situation!)

Changing the diapers of the demented is "caring for the least of these."

Caring for the "least of these" is the work of the Lord.

Therefore, changing Depend diapers is the work of the Lord.

OK. So far, so good. The logic was convincing. All this caretaking was doing the "work of the Lord." But still, I did not have an answer to the question of how this all was not in vain.

Wasn't there some way more meaningful way for me to be spending my time on earth than changing diapers? God could inspire me to write great works of literature, expound on great theological truths, but here I was instead spending my precious time, never to be reclaimed, changing diapers. But then again, there was Jesus, in the hours before His death, washing dirty feet. Wouldn't the time have been better spent in expounding a super-sermon? Maybe a Sermon on the Mount on steroids?

For what seemed like forever, I was given no definitive answer to the question, "How is this not in vain?" The best answer I could articulate was that it was not always ours to understand but just to trust. After all, we were not commanded to "understand the Lord," but "to trust in the Lord." God said caring for the demented was not in vain, and therefore it was not in vain. The end.

Then one day, the perfect answer—fully formed, no thinking required—popped into my head. We are urged, *"Offer your bodies as a living sacrifice, holy and pleasing to God—this is your true and proper worship."* (Romans 12:1).

Lucid

Our bodies, our total selves, are to be a living sacrifice. Notice, there is no mention of perfect bodies and there is no mention of mental capacity—just our bodies, no matter what the condition.

If our bodies are to be a living sacrifice, then they are an offering to God. Offerings to God must never be treated with contempt, as shown in the story of Eli's sons: *"This sin of the young men was very great in the Lord's sight, for they were treating the Lord's offering with contempt."* (1 Samuel 2:17)

Therefore, when we are asked to care for bodies of God's demented children who cannot care for themselves, we must not be contemptuous of these memory-forsaken bodies of their former selves. They are GOD's offerings, and we are honored by God by being asked to care for His "offerings."

Message understood; case closed.

****

December 27, 2012 was Mike's and my forty-fifth wedding anniversary. On this anniversary day—the day that Mike and I had vowed to merge our lives for "better or worse"—I reflected on the meaning of vows and on Psalm 15: 1.4a:

> *Who may dwell in your sacred tent?*
> *Who may live on your holy mountain?*
> *He keeps an oath when it hurts and does not change their mind.*
> *He whoever does these things will not be shaken.*

This anniversary day—day 16,020 of living with Mike—started off with me being urinated on.

A thought occurred to me about how no one ever really talks to engaged couples about what the "worse" of better or worse might

No Sugar Added!

entail! The emphasis is always on the better! I thought that maybe I could write a "realistic" lesson plan for a premarital course!

My lesson would start with:

> *When times are good, be happy*
> *But when times are bad, consider this:*
> *God has made one as well as the other.*
> *Therefore, no one can discover anything about their future.*
> —Ecclesiastes 7:14

The day ended with a perfect example of "worse" to put in my "lesson plan"—a very novel caretaker's injury.

I was changing Mike's diapers while getting him ready for bed. I made him sit down so that I could pull them off. As I lifted his foot to remove the diapers, they caught on his toenail. I gently pulled to release them. Mike's toenail cracked, flew off, and hit me in the right eye. My first thought was, "Do you think I can apply for workman's compensation for my caretaking injuries?" Thankfully, my eye didn't hurt, so I figured the cornea wasn't scratched. But I decided to wear eye protection when changing diapers in the future!

To be totally honest, I could not write my lesson plans on the "worse" without including lesson plans on the "best." After all, there had been approximately 13,207 very good days living with Mike, and only about 3,595 days that were less than optimal and veering to worse.

One of many possible "best" examples to be included in my hypothetical lesson plan was forcibly brought home to me six months before our forty-fifth wedding anniversary. I was reading one of the many articles that were written after Neal Armstrong died. In that obit, there was a graphic timeline presentation of American human spaceflight accomplishments. And there was my name, mentioning my stay on the Mir space station! And all I could think was, "Thank you, Mike. Thank you for your total, unwavering, generous support over the years as your wife chased after her childhood fantasy of living in space."

For a Father's Day present to his dad while our son was in high school, Michael had written a poem that said it all.

The Hero

He lets her go
He lets her live
Though it's him who bears the cross
She circles round
Draws the crowd
And only he feels loss
"Isn't she grand?"
"A real hero she is"
"And not an arrogant bone"
But fools in awe
Don't see the truth
Behind her brilliant glow
For he sits alone
Keeps running the home
Not one bit of glory he seeks
For those who seek glory
Are not the true heroes
It's those who let them seek.

And then there was the evening of this anniversary, which was the 16,802th day that Mike and I had been living together. As I stood outside in the deep darkness of the night, I heard tortured sobbing coming from the bedroom where Mike was sitting. I went

No Sugar Added!

back in. Mike was sitting on the edge of the bed, shaking with heaving sobs, snot streaming from both nostrils. I didn't know what to do. Mike, of course, had no words. I, too, had no words. I sat beside him and put my arm around his shoulders. We sat there, sobbing together. Forty-six years of marriage and this was what we could do together—sob.

Chapter 5

2014: Hospice

*I will repay you for the years the locusts have eaten—
The great locust and the young locust,
The other locusts and the locust swarm—
My great army that I sent among you.
You will have plenty to eat, until you are full
You will praise the name of the Lord your God,
Who has worked wonders for you;
Never again will my people be shamed.
—Joel 2:25–26*

The day came in early January 2014 when I could no longer get Mike out of bed. I could pull him into a sitting position, but I could not get him to stand. I had to get him into a sitting position and then hold him there in order to eat and drink. I had to change him while he was lying down. I put pads under him and rolled him to one side and then the other to get him cleaned and changed. It

No Sugar Added!

was hard. One of the girls would come over to help when she could. It was much easier to clean Mike and to get him dry with two people working together than just one.

Then I discovered the power of "music to change by"!

When I smelled the task before me, my first thought was, "What music should I change by?"

Generally, the selection was trumpets blaring (on full volume, of course) "When the Roll is Called Up Yonder." So appropriate for the task!

Every time Mike screamed "Oh God, oh God!" as I rolled him from side to side, I shouted back, "Thank you, God, for providing Mike with such stellar caretaking!"

At this point, I really didn't have much trouble moving Mike around on the bed. (My definition of easy was not hurting my back.)

One day, the thought occurred to me, "Shannon, you are either one really strong woman, or Mike has lost a lot of weight." The answer, of course, was that Mike had lost a lot of weight.

What with all the music and the shouting, changing Mike morphed into a marvelous, Pentecostal, charismatic, worship service. Every so often during the "service," Mike would holler, "Jackass!" I had never, in over forty-six years of living with Mike, heard him utter that word. So, I figured it was proof that Mike was speaking in tongues!

I decided that no book on Dementia Caretaking Tips would be complete without a chapter titled "Glorious Worship—Dementia Style!"

After one such early morning "service," I looked at all the closed doors up and down our dark street and wondered, "What is really going on behind them?" No one would have guessed what was going on behind my burnt orange front door this morning! And then I thought that maybe I should write an answer to the question

Lucid

posed by a song that was popular when I was in high school, "What's Behind the Green Door?"

Keeping Mike clean and dry as he lay on the bed was extremely stressful. I was worried that Mike would develop bedsores if I could not keep him dry. I was aware that the first person who was ever diagnosed with Alzheimer's had died from deep bedsores that had become infected. I did not want that to happen to Mike. A hospital bed would make my job so much easier. I needed a hospital bed. No, I yearned for a hospital bed! I looked on the internet. They were prohibitively expensive.

I was also extremely stressed because I wanted to make sure that I was doing everything that I could for Mike. For instance, I wanted him to have a flu shot. There was no way that I could get Mike to the doctor. I had taken him to the doctor for his annual checkup right after I had started being Mike's full-time caretaker. Shani went with me. It was a horrible experience. We got him into the van, into the elevator, and then into the office. The aide came in to take his blood pressure. Mike fought her off with flailing fists and kicking feet. She could not get close to him to take his temperature. The doctor came in. He could not get close enough to listen to Mike's heart or lungs. I asked about medication to help Mike not be so agitated. The doctor said that such medications were not an option. They were contraindicated because they shortened a person's life span. The checkup was over. We maneuvered Mike back to the car, home, and into the house. Shani said, "I will never again help take Dad in for useless checkups." I agreed.

And, incidentally, neither of us realized, as we helped Mike from the van into the house, that this was the last time that Mike would ever leave home alive.

I still had not given up on Mike getting a flu shot, so I asked the local druggist if Mike and I could stop at the drive-through prescription window and someone could run out and give him a flu shot as he sat in the car and I held his arms, but I was told that he would have to come inside the drug store. Shots were not dispensed at the drive-through window.

In despair, I prayed, "Lord, what now? I don't have a clue as to what to do!"

The answer Jahaziel gave to King Jehoshaphat as he was waiting to be annihilated by the vast army headed his way popped into my mind: *"March out against them, you will not have to fight this battle. Take your positions; stand firm and see the deliverance the Lord gives you."* (2 Chronicles 20:17)

The answer to my despairing prayer seemed obvious. I was to act. And then I was to wait on the Lord. I was to accept the Lord's answer. Of course, that was much easier said than done!

I acted. I surfed the internet. There were companies that sent doctors out to the house. Even if our insurance did not cover "house calls," I would have been happy to pay for a house call myself just for the peace of mind of knowing that we were doing all that we could for Mike. I called the various companies. I could not find any that was willing to deal with a patient with dementia. Finally, in desperation, I decided to investigate hospice possibilities. There was information on the internet that listed the requirements for a person with dementia to be admitted to hospice. In my humble opinion, Mike certainly met all the requirements—and then some! He did not talk, and he could do no daily self-care activities. He needed help eating. He was totally incontinent. I called a hospice company and explained my dilemma. I said that I knew that we needed a doctor's orders to be admitted to hospice but that I could not get Mike to a doctor, and that I had not been able to find a doctor who would come out to the house in order to evaluate Mike to see if he qualified for hospice. The person I talked to said she would talk to her supervisor and call me back. I heard nothing for a couple of weeks and figured that—once again—I had hit a dead end.

Then, after two weeks, she called back! She said the staff had discussed my situation and that they had agreed to send out their head nurse to evaluate Mike. If the nurse thought that Mike qualified, he would recommend to the hospice doctor that Mike be admitted to hospice.

The nurse came out. He asked how they could help. I said I was planning on taking care of Mike at home and just wanted assurance that I was doing all I could do for him. If Mike developed bedsores, I wanted to know someone to call to help me manage them so that Mike was not in any pain. Ideally, I wanted tips to keep bedsores from developing in the first place.

We went into the bedroom where Mike had been in bed for a month. We pulled Mike into a sitting position. The nurse tried to interact with Mike. Mike tried to lash out with his fists and would not support himself in a sitting position. And of course, there were no verbal responses to any of the nurse's questions.

The nurse finished examining Mike and asked, "How can we help you?"

"Is Mike eligible for hospice?" I asked.

"He certainly is," the nurse replied. "He cannot do any of the self-care items on the list."

"But he can still walk—he just won't."

"Walking is not on the list," the nurse pointed out. "So how can we help?"

"What I am in desperate need of is a hospital bed, a Do Not Resuscitate order (DNR), and a number to call if something physical happens to Mike and he is in pain."

The nurse whipped out his cell phone and ordered a hospital bed. He hung up and said, "The bed will be here this afternoon.

No Sugar Added!

And I will see that the DNR is also delivered to you this afternoon. Are there any medications that you need to have refilled?"

"No. Mike is not taking anything except the probiotics that I get over the counter." It seemed very strange to me that Mike was visibility wasting away in front of us, but all his vital signs were good, and he required no prescription medication.

The nurse filled out several forms, called the hospice doctor to let him know that Mike was admitted to hospice, and then told me that a hospice nurse would be coming every week to check up on Mike. I asked if our Blue Cross policy covered hospice. He then told me that Medicare part A covered hospice 100 percent. He said that someone would come out and help me bathe Mike, but then he agreed with me that that arrangement would not work very well because Mike could only be cleaned when he was amenable, and that time could not be predicted. The nurse also said that Medicare would pay for disposable diapers, but I said that I would continue to pay for Depend diapers myself. They worked great, and I had not had much success with cheaper brands. After all, Mike deserved the best—including top-of-the-line disposable diapers.

Just like that, all the forms were complete and signed, and Mike was officially enrolled in hospice. As promised, the hospital bed and the DNR arrived that very afternoon.

The next morning, as the girls and I were sitting at the kitchen table and planning our weekly schedule, we looked up and were flabbergasted to see Mike amble through the living area and then continue to roam around the house. We looked at each other and asked simultaneously, "Does Dad walking mean he will be kicked out of hospice? Will the hospital bed be taken away?"

****

Lucid

After the hospital bed had arrived, all the grandkids came over and had a great time raising and lowering the bed and moving it around the bedroom. Having a hospital bed made changing Mike so much easier. He did not stay in the hospital bed all the time, because I got him up and into his recliner. Sometimes he would get out of the recliner and pace back and forth. Sometimes he would lay down on the regular bed that was still in the room. I knew that it was good for him to move around. I did not want him lying in one position for too long. I did not want bedsores to develop. I dreaded the possibility of bedsores. I did not want to see Mike in excruciating pain, especially if keeping him moving and changing his position would prevent it from happening.

The hospital bed had another huge advantage. It enabled me to get Mike into bed by myself when I found him on the floor.

I purchased an inflatable mattress that was double the height of most inflatable mattresses. When I found Mike on the floor and after I checked him to make sure he was not hurt and nothing was broken, I rolled out the deflated mattress next to him. Because the floors were laminate, if he was not located where I could get the mattress, I could just pull him near to it. Because the floor was laminate, it was easy to slide him to a better position. Then I just rolled Mike over to his side, pushed the mattress under him, and inflated it. In no time he was lying on a nice, soft "bed." The next step was to lower the hospital bed to its lowest position and put it next to the mattress. Then I could sit on the hospital bed, wrap my arms around Mike, and roll us over onto the hospital bed. I would then get off the bed and raise it to a good height so that I could pull Mike into a standing position to change him. If Mike was not in the mood for that, I could change him as he lay there. When I could not get him up to go to his recliner, I could raise him into a sitting position so that he could eat and drink in the bed. Who would have ever thought that an inanimate object like a hospital bed could have filled me with such gratitude!

Phil was Mike's older brother. He had been diagnosed with Alzheimer's several years after Mike had been diagnosed, and it was very interesting to compare Mike and his brother as they each traveled the dementia trail. Phil had never married and had no children, and so Anita, his niece who lived in the same area that he did, took over responsibility for him. She found an assisted living place where he could live and then, when his resources ran out, she did all the paperwork to get him into a Medicaid room. She was the person who was called when Phil needed something. At the first place he lived, he was found on the floor one morning. He was immediately sent to the emergency room. Anita called and told me about the incident.

Phil was kept in the hospital for observation, and Anita was very frustrated because they would not discharge him without a CAT scan because he was not talking. Anita tried to explain that because of his dementia, he no longer talked. The hospital insisted on Phil being evaluated by a speech therapist. The evaluation confirmed that he did not talk. Unfortunately, because he had fallen, the place where Phil had been living would not take him back. Anita had to find a new place. Because he was on Medicaid and totally without any financial resources, this process, at great expense to taxpayers, was repeated for Phil every time he was found on the floor. On the other hand, because Mike was being cared for by his family, every time he was found on the floor, it just involved family members assessing the situation and—seeing no physical damage—getting him back into bed. There were no 911 calls, no emergency room visits, and no extra cost to anyone.

Thinking about how nice it was to have a hospital bed in our home got me thinking about what I was most thankful for as I cared for Mike. It was a strange list. I thanked the Lord for the hospital

Lucid

bed, for laminate floors, for a great washing machine, for a plethora of "finger foods," for probiotics, for daughters who were willing to be full-time caretaking partners, for a son who was totally supportive even if separated from us by thousands of miles, for strong sons-in-law, for sons-in-law willing to stay with a demented father-in-law, for Depend adult diapers, for my good health, for a house with a floor plan amenable to caretaking a person with dementia, for a DNR order, for the weekly visits of the hospice nurses, for video cameras that could let me watch Mike on my phone when I was not at home, for daily visits of lively for grandchildren filling the house with songs and laughter, for ice cream, and for Amazon Prime.

Amazon Prime? Yes, Amazon Prime!

It was amazing how online shopping simplified caretaking. Depend diapers were delivered to my front door every month. When we needed a refrigerator lock, we found the perfect one online—ditto for door locks and gate locks. Sheets for the hospital bed, nonskid socks, and disposable mouth cleaners were all just a click away. There was no need to go from store to store to search for products that would make things just a little easier. Everything needed was online—and when we purchased one thing, up popped more very useful suggestions.

When Mike got enrolled in hospice, our life took on a different rhythm. It was very comforting to have the DNR order, to have a number to call if something happened to Mike, and a number to call if he needed pain medications. I would receive help to keep him as free of pain as possible. It was a huge relief.

A nurse came by at least once a week. The nurse would measure Mike's arm as a way of estimating his declining weight, take his blood pressure, and listen to his heart and lungs—that is, if Mike would let that happen. Then the nurse would fill out all the required forms and tell me what a good job I was doing. It surprised me how much it meant to me to be told I was doing a good job. I needed that affirmation.

The nurses, without exception, were professional and very kind. In talking to them, I was surprised to learn how many had had close relatives with dementia that they had taken care of at home.

I found myself looking forward to their visits. Invariably, they would ask some questions about who Mike had been before he had dementia. Most importantly, they treated Mike with respect, as an individual of great value.

After one of their weekly visits, I realized that if a miracle occurred and Mike became un-demented—yes, like a demented Rip Van Winkle—Mike would instantly find himself in an un-demented world where he had:

never used a cell phone
never read an e-book
never owned a Kindle
never used GPS
never knew the space shuttle had stopped launching
never knew he had gone to a Baptist church for three years
never knew that his wife no longer worked at NASA
never knew all his grandchildren
The list could go on and on!

****

The grandkids were constantly in and out of the house, almost on a daily basis. We explained to them that their grandfather was in hospice and what that meant. It was very interesting to watch each of the grandchildren process this information as they watched the final stage of their grandfather's life play out before them.

Shortly after Mike entered hospice, when Brooke was five, this letter from her, showed up in my mailbox.

Lucid

Grandma,
I love you so much that you are the best Grandma I ever had so I love you super, super much. You are the best I ever had. I know your favorite animals are birds. I know you love your husband grandpa. I know he will die soon but you'll still love him.
Love Brooke

I took Brooke and Brianna to the store to buy new school outfits. They both picked out locket necklaces instead. As we were leaving the store, they asked me, "Grandma, do you know why we needed these necklaces?"

"No," I replied.

"Because we are going to put a picture of Grandpa in them," they said. "He might be dead soon, and we don't want to forget what he looked like. That is why we really needed these lockets!"

So, there you have it!

Then there was the day that Brianna, Paige, and Brooke burst into the house while they were discussing Resurrection and the Rapture. They were talking about getting to see Scott—our first grandchild, their brother and cousin, who died at birth.

Paige said, "Scott never did anything bad, and he never did anything good, but he is in Heaven waiting for us. We will all have new bodies. Even Grandpa will have a new body!"

Brianna replied, "Well, really, we will be happy if Grandpa just gets a new brain—that is what he really needs!"

****

Caring for a baby and caring for a demented person have many similarities. There is changing diapers, preparing appropriate food, no verbal communication, and a strong focus on keeping them safe

No Sugar Added!

and comfortable. However, because of the expected outcomes when one looks into the future, the emotions and the rewards are polar opposites—think day and night, think joy and sadness.

When you care for a baby, each day brings its rewards of new things learned and of the celebration of little changes that mark progress toward independence and the realization of selfhood. You are caring not only for the present crying baby but for the potential of the person that baby will become. Every day, you see tiny signs of that emerging person.

Caring for the demented each day brings the desolation of loss of some ability that the person no longer has and the dissolving of the person who was into the nonperson who now is. The thread of continuity is gone. There is no resemblance to the person held in the caretaker's memory with the person being cared for on a daily basis. And you wonder: Is there a point where the person who once was is now no longer? What happened to that person? Whom are you caring for? You try to connect some dots and find something you can hang on to and say, "This is the person I married so many years ago," but there is nothing left. And then, even any physical resemblance to the former person disappears.

There are caretakers of babies. There are caretakers of those with dementia. A quick perusal of the job descriptions for each look remarkably similar. Both jobs require that the object of care be kept fed, kept clean, kept safe, and blanketed in love. Both jobs require total commitment. Both jobs are 24/7. And yet, the two tasks could not be perceived by both society and caretakers themselves more differently—and, in fact, could not be more different. I laughed when I realized what an affinity I had with Sarah, Abraham's wife. Like her, I was way past childbearing age, but found myself awash in diapers and bottles!

People yearn to be the caretakers of babies. No one yearns to be the caretaker of a person with dementia. The thought of taking care of a baby fills most people with joy. The thought of taking care of the demented fills most people with dread. Fabulous sums of money are spent by some people for the privilege of having a baby and becoming that baby's caretaker. Fabulous sums of money are spent by some people for the privilege of not having to be a demented person's caretaker. Taking care of a baby fills a person with the satisfaction of his or her life being spent well. Taking care of a demented person fills a person with a sense of his or her life being utterly wasted. There is support available—and generally easy to find—to help a caretaker to care for a baby. There is very little support—and what little exists is very difficult to find and access—for the caretaker of the demented. Society values the caretakers of babies. Society does not value the caretakers of the demented. The church highly values babies and their caretakers. Generally, a demented person is not valued by the church, and the needs of their caretakers are ignored.

A baby is like spring—the season of abundant hope. Caring for a baby is daily caring for the promise of spring unfolding into the savory fruits of summer as well as the anticipation of summer unfolding into fall's bountiful harvest. (Generally, the hopeful visions for a baby end with fall, and no thought is given to the inevitability of winter.)

A demented person is winter—the season of no hope. While caring for the demented, there is no anticipation of savory summer fruits or bountiful fall harvests. There is only the anticipation of continuous winter storms, howling ever more powerfully—a blizzard of neurofibrillary tangles through which no path can be shoveled.

A baby is a bud—"grace here is glory in the bud," as Alexander MacLaren wrote in *Expositions of Holy Scripture*. The baby's caretaker is astonished and amazed on a daily basis, watching as the bud blossoms forth—bit by bit, day by day. The baby's caretaker prays, "Thank you, God, for the privilege of being a part of this unfolding miracle."

A demented person is but an empty husk, twisting furiously in the winter winds—a husk so shriveled and distorted that it is impossible to recognize the fruit that was once housed within it. The caretaker of the demented is horrified by the shriveling of the husk and prays, "Oh God, how long? How long?"

The baby's caretaker marvels about the "God of Creation" who *"knew and formed me in my mother's womb."* (Psalm 139:13)

The demented person's caretaker is scandalized by unbidden thoughts that the "God the Potter" destroys and casts onto the trash heap of life a vessel of his creation.

Caretakers of babies are rarely bothered by philosophical doubts concerning the purpose of their work. Even when totally overwhelmed with the caring process, they see the value of it. They exalt in a first smile, a first word, or a first step.

Caretakers of the demented, always totally overwhelmed, wonder daily, even hourly, "Why?" They search for purpose but find only purposelessness in their work. They despair at the expressionless features, at the loss of all words, and at the loss of locomotion.

Caretakers of the demented often find themselves feeling that their lives are being lived for no purpose. They are acutely aware of their lives, like sand in an hourglass, trickling away. The caretaker can't help but think that life is being poured out for no purpose—just being wasted. Their constant thought is, I could be doing so many great things for the Lord if not tied down by all this caring—caring that is not even appreciated!

When Paul the Apostle felt that his life was being poured out, he did not think of his life as being wasted but that it was an act of worship that he offered to God.

Lucid

"But even as I am being poured out like a drink offering on the sacrifice and service coming from your faith, I am glad and rejoice with all of you." (Phil 2:17)

The Old and New Testaments are replete with examples of oils, perfumes, wines, and water of great value that, instead of being consumed for what the culture would say were very worthy projects, were poured out to worship God—acts that were, incidentally, condemned as being wasteful by the spectators.

Remember David pouring out the water he longed for instead of drinking it after it had been brought to him at great risk to the lives of his friends? Remember Mary Magdalene pouring out perfume, which was worth a year's wages, onto the feet of Jesus?

All this pouring out of these offerings appeared to be wasteful, but they were acts of worship.

Pouring out a life into caring seems wasteful in the eyes of society, but isn't it just being poured out as an offering to God and—as such—is an act of worship to Him? *"Rather in humility value others above yourselves, not looking to your own interests but each of you to the interests of others."* (Phil 2:3b–4)

And then, one day, while caring for Mike, I had an epiphany. Suddenly, I had an answer to the question, "Why?" and glimpsed the deep joy, purpose, and privilege of caring for the demented.

To me, Mike was a disappeared person. Over ten years, I had watched him, in discontinuous steps, fall from one plateau down to the next, always dissolving with no connection to a past memory of the Mike we knew.

My epiphany was that it really made no difference if I did not know or could not find Mike in the person I was caring for, because God knew. God had promised that he would never forsake Mike, and somehow God was there with Mike.

No Sugar Added!

Psalm for the Demented

I can never get away from your presence!
If I go up to heaven, you are there
If I go down to the grave, you are there
If I ride the wind of the morning
If I dwell in the farthest oceans, even there your hand will guide me
And your strength will support me
I could ask the darkness to hide me
And the light around me to become night
But even in darkness I cannot hide from you
To you the night shines as bright as day
Darkness or light are the same to you.
—Psalm 139:7–12

Because Mike had answered yes to the invitation of Jesus to follow Him and to be a citizen in the Kingdom of God, the Holy Spirit dwelt in Mike. As Saint Paul so richly proclaimed in I Corinthians 3:16, *"Don't you know that you yourselves are God's temple and that God's Spirit dwells in your midst?"* Mike no longer knew anybody, much less God. But God knew Mike. The presence of the Holy Spirit and Mike's body being the Temple of God was not changed by the fact that Mike no longer knew any of us and that he no longer knew God. God knew Mike. (Reread the above psalm for the demented!) Mike's body was the Temple of God. And when I fed Mike, shaved Mike, or cleaned Mike, I was taking care of God's temple. Twenty-four hours a day and seven days a week, I was caring for the Temple of God.

Every Christmas, we read the story of Anna—the widowed, childless woman who spent every day at the temple in Jerusalem, praying to and worshipping God. And then one day, she saw Mary and Joseph holding baby Jesus in their arms. To all who were there and looking forward to the redemption of Jerusalem, she preached the good news about this child. God used an old, widowed woman who had spent her life caring for His temple to be the first to loudly proclaim the good news about the baby Jesus. She would soon die in peace, after a life well spent.

Pondering the story of Anna, I understood that the years of caring for Mike were not years of waste and desolation but years of purpose and praise—years dedicated to the caring of God's temple.

I prayed a prayer of thanksgiving: "Thank you, Lord, for letting me understand how I was serving you."

Realizing that I was caring for the Temple of God changed everything. Yes, keeping Mike safe and clean was still very hard, but it was now labor with a holy purpose.

We often say, "God's ways, not our ways." But let's be honest—doesn't it take us a little by surprise when we see evidence of it?

I remembered the prayer I had prayed so many times, as I got older, asking God to use me. I reminded God how He had used Abraham, Moses, and Samson, not letting their age be a barrier to serving Him. Now, I was realistic. I did not expect God to use me to lead a group of grumbling complainers through the Red Sea, but I was quite capable of doing many things, and I prayed that God would just show me where He wanted me to serve Him, because I would gladly serve. And God answered my prayers. God showed me Mike's need! (Incidentally, doesn't God have a great sense of humor?)

God had answered my prayers and provided me with great work to do in the Kingdom of God. It was not what I would have ever thought of doing. It was not what I would ever have considered as Kingdom Work. And not only did God give me work to accomplish, God enabled me to understand that I was doing His work.

Chapter 6

November–December 2014:

The End

Precious on the sight of the Lord is the death of his faithful servants.
—Psalm 116:15a

In early November, Mike, once again, stopped walking around the house. He just lay in bed, except that now he was light enough so that I could slide the recliner next to the hospital bed, grab him around the waist, and pull him into it. It just made me feel better to have him "sitting" up in the recliner for a good part of the day. It was also easier to feed him and get him to drink when he was sitting in the recliner than it was when he was lying in the hospital bed. With the help of the girls, I could still get him standing to be changed, and we would move him from the "normal" bed to the hospital bed to the recliner and back again. I did this because it seemed to me that Mike would be in a slightly different position in each of these, thereby decreasing the chance of bed sores. To us, it appeared that he had reverted to being like he was in January, when we first contacted hospice. He was still eating, but mostly just ice cream, popsicles, grilled cheese sandwiches, bananas, and a large glass of orange juice every morning.

Michael came home for Thanksgiving. Mike and I had so much to be thankful for—even if he no longer was aware of it. All our children were home, and eight grandchildren were constantly running in and out of the house over the Thanksgiving break.

Sunday, December 14

Mike had not gotten up on his own since shortly before Thanksgiving. On Sunday afternoon, December 14, the girls were at the house and the twins were running around. Suddenly, we noticed that Mike was in the living room, sitting on the couch. Totally surprised, the girls and I asked each other, "How did that happen? Did he teleport?" We had not expected to ever see Mike out the bedroom again.

Davey walked up to the side of his grandpa. I told Davey to get closer, because I wanted to take a picture. He got a slightly uncomfortable look on his face and refused. I took a picture with him where he was. This was the first time that either Davey or Danny had not been excited to see their grandpa. Up to this moment, they both had always been eager to hold Mike's hand, get close, hug his legs, and help bring food to him. I told the girls that this was a sign that Davey was growing up. For the first time, he realized that his grandpa was "strange."

That evening, I was sitting in the den, reading. Everyone else was gone. I had just checked on Mike. He was lying on the normal bed in the bedroom. The girls had helped me change him before they left. I heard a loud crash and a scream. I ran into the bedroom and there was Mike, lying on his back on the floor and screaming. I calmed him down and checked him over. No broken bones. I scooted him closer to the bed and sat him up on the floor. I sat on the bed, wrapped my arms around him, and then—with a heft, a heave, and then with us both rolling together—got him up onto the bed. I rolled him off me and got him comfortable. (By this time, Mike was small enough and light enough for me to lift him without help.)

The next morning, a Monday, Mike was still in bed, but he was curled up in a fetal position. When I tried to straighten him, he screamed in agony. Seeing her dad like this disturbed Kawai greatly. She kept insisting that his leg was broken or out of joint and begged me to do something. Mike did not respond as if in pain to any examination of his legs or joints—only to attempts to straighten him out and make him comfortable. But then I did something I had not done before. I got the morphine that had been delivered on the first day Mike entered hospice, put in the refrigerator, and never been touched since. I gave Mike the recommended dosage by dribbling it slowly from a syringe into his mouth. Soon it appeared that his pain had lessened. Kawai and I then got Mike into the hospital bed by rolling it close to the big bed and lifting Mike into it.

From this point until Christmas, Mike stayed in the hospital bed. Because he stayed in the fetal position, I could keep the rails on the hospital bed up to keep him from rolling out without being concerned that he would get trapped by them if he tried to get out of bed. That had always been a concern when he was still flailing around. Now, we cleaned and changed him in the hospital bed.

I set up a watch station in the bedroom. I had a chair, a lamp, books, and a battery-operated Christmas candle. I slept on the normal bed and spent all my time in the bedroom with Mike.

Lucid

Wednesday, December 17

Mike's niece called and said that Mike's brother Phil had died. He had fallen at the nursing home and was sent to the emergency room. The surgeon on duty wanted to do exploratory surgery. Mike's niece, backed up by her sister, said absolutely not. He should not be subjected to that much trauma. They insisted that Phil was to be admitted to hospice. He was put in the hospice portion of the hospital on the cancer floor and died later that night. The surgeon insisting on the invasive surgery apologized to Anita for the pressure he had exerted when Phil arrived at the hospital.

Friday, December 19

Mike's hospice nurse stopped by in the morning. I met her at the door with the lime Popsicle that I was going to give to Mike in my hand. I put the Popsicle back into the freezer.

Michelle, the nurse, said it was time to give Mike the drug Lorazepam, which is a sedative. She showed me how to dissolve it in a spoon, draw it up into a syringe, and then dribble it into Mike's mouth. She also showed me how to place pillows between Mike's legs so that they would not touch each other as he lay curled on his side.

I asked her how long someone could live in the condition that Mike was now in. She said maybe a month, but only seven to fourteen days after he stopped eating. I specifically asked if Mike would die before Christmas, and she said she did not think so. We agreed that an aide would come and help me bathe Mike the next week.

No Sugar Added!

After Michelle left, I could not get Mike to eat or drink anything. The Popsicle just rolled around in his mouth, melted, and dribbled out the side. A bite of sandwich just sat in his mouth until I removed it. Mike had suddenly lost the ability to swallow. I had an overpowering panic reaction. We must DO something! A feeding tube! That was the answer! I must get a feeding tube inserted! (It was at that moment that I understood why family members insisted, against all reason, that something be done when watching someone they love enter the terminal phase of life.) I took a deep breath and prayed, "Lord, provide the strength needed for the next phase of caring for Mike. Thank you"

Kawai, the kids, and I went to a Trans-Siberian Express concert that evening. Shani stayed with Mike. She was very distressed that she could not get him to swallow anything.

When we got back, I started the routine of trying to turn Mike every two to three hours. Anywhere his body was in contact with the bed, it turned red. If a part of his body touched the bed for too long, the skin split and there were raw places. Turning Mike often and changing his position kept the skin from splitting, but Mike screamed in pain whenever he was turned. I gave him morphine and lorazepam thirty minutes before I moved him, and I tried to keep his lips moist at all times.

Saturday, December 20

Before Shani went to Walmart, she called and asked if there was anything I needed. I asked her to get some more lip chap for Mike's cracked lips. Later that day, she brought it over and said, "Merry Christmas, Dad. I guess this the only present I can give you that you can actually use."

Monday, December 22

The hospice aide came over at seven in the evening and "bathed" Mike. She used Mike's electric shaver and got Mike shaved very well. She did a better job shaving Mike than I had been able to do. After she finished, Mike looked downright spiffy! She pointed out that if I kept the foot of the bed slightly raised, Mike would not slide down and I would not have to keep pulling him up in the bed. That was a very useful tip.

I continued to spend all my free time in the bedroom, reading and making sure I turned Mike often.

Wednesday, December 24—Christmas Eve

I did not go to the evening service at church, but everyone came over afterward for our traditional, light Christmas Eve supper. After everyone left, I cleared up and got the table set for Christmas dinner. Everything was ready by nine. I slept in the big recliner, which I could pull close to Mike's bed, in the bedroom with Mike. I turned him and changed him at midnight. The Christmas globe battery operated candle was on like it had been every evening for the last week. There was great peace and calm in the room.

Thursday, December 25—Christmas Day

At daybreak, I woke up. It was Christmas morning! I checked on Mike. He was sleeping so peacefully that I did not have the heart to move him. I told him (and myself) that his being at peace was more important than keeping his skin from splitting. Not moving him was my Christmas gift to him. At this point, what difference did it make if a few bedsores started to develop? I got dressed and stood by Mike's side. It was not yet time to put the ham in the oven. I held his hand. I noticed his jaw move from side to side, and then there was a very shallow breath.

"Oh," I said. "You are leaving us." Two more shallow breaths followed and then—just like that—Mike was gone. Mike's pain had ended. I continued to stand there in peace. Then I whispered, "Thank you, Lord, for taking care of Mike." When I finally glanced at the clock, it was nine thirty on Christmas morning.

"Those who walk uprightly enter into peace; they find rest as they lie in death." (Isaiah 57:2)

I was not sure how soon rigor mortis would set in, so I quickly moved Mike to wash and clean him. Then I dressed him in brand new underwear—no more demeaning diapers—and put brand new sweatpants and a sweatshirt on him. After Mike was clean and dressed in new clothes, I texted the kids to let them know that their father had died.

I called the hospice number, and the on-call operator said she would inform the on-call nurse. Soon the on-call nurse, Jodie, who had come out to see Mike early in his time with hospice, called and said that she would be out as soon as she had showered and dressed. I said there was no rush.

The girls came over. We waited. After a while, they said that we might as well put away everything that was set out for Christmas dinner. So, we did. It was faster putting away the green Frankoma pottery and folding the poinsettia Christmas tablecloths than it had been to set them up the night before. We folded up the tables and put them back in the garage. Then we sat and waited some more.

We sat in the living room and gazed out the window at the day, which was a picture of perfection. There wasn't a cloud in the perfectly blue sky. All was totally calm—no breeze, no cars, and no people.

Lucid

Jodie, the hospice nurse, came at about noon. She verified that Mike had died and then sat down to do the paperwork. She asked if we had picked out a funeral home.

I said, "Not really, but I had thought about—" She interrupted me and gave a recommendation. I said, "OK, that's fine with us," She called the funeral home. They said it would be a while before they came to get Mike because there were four families ahead of us. I told Jodie that was fine. There was no rush. Jodie called the hospice doctor to report Mike's death, and then she called the equipment people to arrange for the hospital bed to be picked up the next day. After that, she said we had to get rid of all the drugs. She had to count and measure the amounts that were left before we disposed of them. So, I got them, and she wrote down the amount of morphine remaining. She said that she did not have cat litter with her to dispose of the morphine and the lorazepam, so I should just flush them down the toilet. I flushed the drugs as she watched.

She then sat and started to wait with us for the people from the funeral home to arrive. I told her that she did not need to wait. The girls and I would just wait together, so she left. The girls and I continued to sit and wait. As we waited, the house had never seemed so peaceful. We were discussing the oddity of Dad dying on Christmas, and Kawai said, "What a great Christmas present for Dad. Present with the Lord, and no longer demented." (Because she said that, I later had a good line to use when writing to inform friends of Mike's death.)

Finally, at about three, a white hearse pulled up in front of the house. Two men with a stretcher came in. They introduced themselves and then I introduced them to Mike. The girls and I waited in the front room for them to put Mike on the stretcher. They wheeled Mike out the front door, out of the house where he had lived for over thirty years, into the sunshine, and into the hearse. Mike was covered with the orange-and-white striped sheet that had been on the bed. They drove off.

The girls then called home and told their families to come over for Christmas supper at around five. We then had a very oddly subdued Christmas supper and gave the kids the presents from Dad and me. Together we cleared the table and stacked the dishes. Everyone then left.

****

I was home alone. For the first time in forty-seven years, I had no one else that I was responsible for.

Thank you, Mike, for all you gave each one of us over the years.

Thank you, Lord, for providing on a daily basis what was needed to care for Mike so that he could die at home, surrounded by his family.

THE END

Made in the USA
Coppell, TX
15 March 2023